Ladies' Home Journal®

100 GREAT

PIE & PASTRY

RECIPES

D0576460

LADIES' HOME JOURNAL™ BOOKS
New York / Des Moines

LADIES' HOME JOURNAL™ BOOKS
An Imprint of Meredith® Books

100 GREAT PIE & PASTRY RECIPES
Editor: Shelli McConnell
Writer/Researcher: Carol Prager
Copy Editor: Jennifer Miller
Associate Art Director: Tom Wegner
Food Stylist: Mariann M. Sauvion
Prop Stylist: Betty Alfenito
Photographer: Steven Mark Needham
Electronic Production Coordinator: Paula Forest
Production Manager: Douglas Johnston

Vice President and Editorial Director: Elizabeth P. Rice
Executive Editor: Kay M. Sanders
Art Director: Ernest Shelton
Managing Editor: Christopher Cavanaugh

President, Book Group: Joseph J. Ward
Vice President, Retail Marketing: Jamie L. Martin
Vice President, Direct Marketing: Timothy Jarrell

LADIES' HOME JOURNAL®
Publishing Director and Editor-in-Chief: Myrna Blyth
Food Editor: Jan Turner Hazard
Associate Food Editors: Susan Sarao Westmoreland, Lisa Brainerd

On the cover: Chocolate-Peanut Butter Ice Cream Pie, page 61.

Meredith Corporation
Chairman of the Executive Committee: E.T. Meredith III
Chairman of the Board and Chief Executive Officer: Jack D. Rehm
President and Chief Operating Officer: William T. Kerr

All of us at Ladies' Home Journal Books are dedicated to providing you with the ideas and recipe information you need to create wonderful foods. We guarantee your satisfaction with this book for as long as you own it. We welcome your comments and suggestions. Please write to us at: Ladies' Home Journal Books, RW 240, 1716 Locust Street, Des Moines, IA 50309-3023.

To ensure that Ladies' Home Journal recipes meet the highest standards for flavor, nutrition, appearance and reliability, we test them a minimum of three times in our Test Kitchen. That makes for quality you can count on.

If you would like to order additional copies of any of our books, call 1-800-678-2803 or check with your local bookstore.

© Copyright 1995 by Meredith Corporation, Des Moines, Iowa.
All rights reserved. Printed in Hong Kong.
First Edition. Printing Number and Year: 5 4 3 2   99 98 97 96
Library of Congress Catalog Card Number: 95-75622
ISBN: 0-696-20125-9

Pies, Glorious Pies

There's nothing more sweetly satisfying than a slice of homemade pie. Filled with peak-season fruit, creamy chocolate, smooth custard, or mile-high chiffon, each bite will please your palate. In this collection of the best pies and tarts around, there are blue-ribbon winners from country fairs, specialties submitted by chef's from across the country, and sophisticated and elegant tarts as well as other favorites from the editors at Ladies' Home Journal. Better get baking so you can indulge in a piece of the pie!

CONTENTS

Perfect Pastry

Tender, flaky pastries to use again and again.

Great American Apple Pies

Double-crusted, lattice-topped, and crumb-sprinkled—they're all apple.

The Best of Summer's Pies

Pies to savor when fruits are at their plump and juicy best.

Sweet and Silky Pies

Pudding-, custard-, or ice cream-filled—rich and creamy and oh-so wonderfully dreamy.

PERFECT PIE AND TART PASTRY

Preparing and rolling out homemade pie and tart pastry doesn't have to be intimidating—and with each flaky, buttery bite, you'll know the effort is well worth it.

Cutting in the butter or shortening: Always chill the butter, margarine, or vegetable shortening in advance. Cut the butter into the dry ingredients with a pastry blender or 2 knives until the mixture has lumps the size of small peas. Do not overmix or the pastry will be tough.

Mixing the pastry: Make sure the liquid is cold—if you are using water, chill it with a few ice cubes. Gradually add the liquid, one tablespoon at a time, tossing the mixture lightly with a fork after each addition. Your dough will appear crumbly, but will feel moist. If the pastry is dry, add a little more liquid. (For a tender and flaky pastry, do not add too much liquid or handle the dough more than necessary.)

Rolling out the pastry: Before you get started, if the pastry has been refrigerated, let it stand for 15 minutes at room temperature before rolling it out. We recommend wax paper for rolling, which makes turning and lifting the pastry easier.

Place your pastry disk between 2 lightly floured sheets of wax paper. Place the rolling pin in the center of the pastry and begin to roll away from you. Turn the wax paper a quarter turn and roll, then repeat the process to gently stretch the dough.

If your kitchen is hot, or you're having trouble rolling the dough, refrigerate the pastry until firm.

If the pastry sticks to the paper during rolling, sprinkle it lightly with more flour.

Fluting pie pastry: In a single-crust pie, a simple raised pastry flute helps prevent your filling from overflowing. In a double crust, a fluted edge seals the top and bottom crust together.

For a simple edge, form an even, raised dough edge around the rim of the pie pan, or trim the dough edge even with the edge of the pie pan. Dip the tines of a fork in flour and gently press around the inside edge of dough. (This can also be done with the rounded side of a spoon.)

For a simple scalloped flute, form an even, ¾-inch high dough edge around the rim of the pie pan. Place your right index finger on the outside of the pie rim. Press dough in toward the center of the pie pan while pressing out from the center of the pie plate with your left thumb and index finger, to form a "V" shape. Repeat this process all around the edge of the pie.

Fancy top: Pastry scraps are a wonderful way to create prettier pies. Reroll pastry scraps and use small decorative cutters to cut various shapes. Brush the rim of the pastry shell or the top of a double crust pie with beaten egg or water and attach shapes in a decorative way.

SINGLE FLAKY PASTRY

The combination of butter and shortening gives this all-purpose pie pastry both the flakiness and buttery flavor we all love.

O *Prep time: 10 minutes plus chilling*
Degree of difficulty: easy

1½ **cups all-purpose flour**
¼ **teaspoon salt**
6 **tablespoons cold butter** *or*
     margarine, cut up
2 **tablespoons vegetable shortening**
4 **to 6 tablespoons ice water**

1 Combine the flour and salt in a medium bowl. Gradually add the butter and shortening, tossing gently until all the pieces are coated with flour. With a pastry blender or 2 knives, cut in butter and shortening until mixture resembles coarse crumbs. Add the ice water, 1 tablespoon at a time, tossing vigorously with a fork until the pastry just begins to hold together.

2 On a smooth surface, shape pastry into a ball, kneading lightly if necessary; flatten into a thick disk. Wrap the pastry tightly in plastic wrap and refrigerate for 1 hour or overnight.

3 On a lightly floured surface with a floured rolling pin, roll pastry into a 13-inch circle and fit it into a 9-inch pie pan, letting pastry overhang the edge. Trim pastry leaving a 1-inch overhang. Fold under pastry edge and flute. Fill and bake pie as directed in recipes.

FULLY BAKED FLAKY PASTRY

After removing your baked shell from the oven, cool it completely on a wire rack before filling it.

Freezing time: 20 minutes
Baking time: 20 to 22 minutes

Single Flaky Pastry (recipe, at left)

1 Preheat oven to 425°F. Prick the bottom of Single Flaky Pastry with a fork at ½-inch intervals. Freeze 20 minutes.

2 Line the frozen pastry shell with foil and fill it with dried beans or raw rice. Bake for 12 minutes or until the edges of the pie shell are set. Remove foil and beans. (Keep the beans and rice; they can be used again.) Bake pastry for 8 to 10 minutes more or until deep golden. If the pastry puffs up during baking, prick it again with a fork. Cool completely on a wire rack. (To make ahead, wrap and store the baked pastry at room temperature up to 24 hours or freeze it up to 1 week. If the crust is frozen, thaw it completely, then crisp it in a preheated 350°F. oven for 10 minutes. Cool before filling.)

NOTES

_____
_____
_____
_____
_____
_____
_____

DOUBLE FLAKY PASTRY

Prep time: 10 minutes plus chilling
O *Degree of difficulty: easy*

2   **cups all-purpose flour**
½   **teaspoon salt**
½   **cup cold butter *or* margarine,**
        cut up
¼   **cup vegetable shortening**
4   **to 6 tablespoons ice water**

1 Combine the flour and salt in a large bowl. Gradually add the butter and shortening, tossing gently until all the pieces are coated with flour. With a pastry blender or 2 knives, cut in butter and shortening until mixture resembles coarse crumbs. Sprinkle with the ice water, 1 tablespoon at a time, tossing vigorously with a fork until the pastry just begins to hold together.

2 On a smooth surface, shape pastry into a ball, kneading lightly if necessary. Divide pastry into 2 balls, one slightly larger than the other. Flatten into 2 thick disks. Wrap the pastry tightly in plastic wrap and refrigerate for 1 hour or overnight.

8

OLD-FASHIONED VINEGAR PASTRY

This super-flaky pie crust contains Grandma's secret ingredient—vinegar! (An equal amount of fresh lemon juice will do the same trick.)

Prep time: 10 minutes plus chilling
O *Degree of difficulty: easy*

2   **cups all-purpose flour**
½   **teaspoon salt**
½   **cup cold butter *or* margarine,**
        cut up
3   **tablespoons vegetable shortening**
1   **tablespoon distilled white vinegar**
4   **to 5 tablespoons ice water**

1 Combine the flour and salt in a large bowl. Gradually add the butter and shortening, tossing gently until all the pieces are coated with flour. With a pastry blender or 2 knives, cut in butter and shortening until mixture resembles coarse crumbs. Sprinkle with the vinegar then add the ice water, one tablespoon at a time, tossing vigorously with a fork until the pastry just begins to hold together.

2 On a smooth surface, shape pastry into a ball, kneading lightly if necessary. Divide pastry into 2 balls, 1 slightly larger than the other. Flatten into 2 thick disks. Wrap the pastry tightly in plastic wrap and refrigerate it for 1 hour or overnight. Proceed as directed in recipe.

NOTES

ULTIMATE TART PASTRY

Prep time: 10 minutes plus chilling
Baking time: 26 to 30 minutes
○ *Degree of difficulty: easy*

1¼ **cups all-purpose flour**
⅛ **teaspoon salt**
½ **cup cold unsalted butter, cut up**
   (no substitutions)
3 **tablespoons ice water**

1 Combine the flour and salt in a medium bowl. Gradually add the butter, tossing gently until all pieces are coated with flour. With a pastry blender or 2 knives, cut in the butter until mixture resembles fine crumbs. Add the ice water, 1 tablespoon at a time, tossing vigorously with a fork until the pastry just begins to hold together.

2 On a smooth surface, shape pastry into a ball, kneading lightly if necessary. Flatten into a thick disk. Wrap the pastry tightly in plastic wrap and refrigerate for 1 hour or overnight.

3 Preheat oven to 425°F. On a lightly floured surface with a floured rolling pin, roll the pastry into a 14-inch circle about ⅛-inch thick. Fold pastry in half. Carefully transfer pastry to a 9- or 10-inch tart pan with a removable bottom. Gently press pastry with fingertips along the bottom and up the side of the pan. With scissors, trim pastry to 1 inch above the edge of the pan. Fold overhanging pastry to the inside of crust and gently press edge up to extend ¼ inch above side of pan. Prick the bottom with a fork. Freeze pastry shell for 20 minutes.

4 Line the frozen pastry shell with foil and fill it with dried beans or uncooked rice. Bake 12 minutes. Remove foil and beans. Bake pastry 14 to 16 minutes more or until deep golden. Cool completely on a wire rack. Remove sides of pan. Transfer the pastry to a serving plate and fill as desired.

SAVORY TART PASTRY

Prep time: 10 minutes plus chilling
○ *Degree of difficulty: easy*

1½ **cups all-purpose flour**
½ **teaspoon salt**
¼ **cup cold butter *or* margarine,**
   cut up
2 **tablespoons vegetable shortening**
3 **to 4 tablespoons ice water**

1 Combine the flour and salt in a medium bowl. Gradually add the butter and shortening, tossing gently until all the pieces are coated with flour. With a pastry blender or 2 knives, cut in butter and shortening until mixture resembles fine crumbs. Add the ice water, one tablespoon at a time, tossing vigorously with a fork until the pastry just begins to hold together.

2 On a smooth surface, shape pastry into a ball, kneading lightly if necessary. Flatten into a thick disk. Wrap the pastry tightly in plastic wrap and refrigerate for 30 minutes or overnight. Proceed as directed in recipe.

GREAT AMERICAN

APPLE PIES

Apples, apples, apples...red or green, sweet or tart, they all have a snap with every bite and a special flavor for every pie. We love apple pies open-faced, crumb-topped, and cream- or cheese-filled. Start with classics such as Mom's Classic Apple Pie, Sour Cream Apple Pie, or Dutch Apple Custard Pie. Then for something a little different, try Cranberry-Apple Pie or Molasses Spice Apple Pie. No matter which recipe you try, you can bet it will be as American as apple pie!

VERMONT APPLE PIE

Cheddar cheese, apples, and maple syrup team up so well that Mom's pie will never be quite the same.

Prep time: 25 minutes
Baking time: 60 to 70 minutes
● *Degree of difficulty: moderate*

Pastry
- 2 cups all-purpose flour
- ½ teaspoon salt
- ⅔ cup vegetable shortening
- 1 cup (4 ounces) shredded sharp cheddar cheese
- 6 to 8 tablespoons ice water

Filling
- 9 cups peeled, sliced, tart apples (Granny Smith, Jonathan, *or* Pippin) (8 *or* 9)
- 1 tablespoon fresh lemon juice
- ¾ cup pure maple syrup
- ¼ cup firmly packed brown sugar
- ¼ cup all-purpose flour
- ½ teaspoon cinnamon

1 For pastry, combine the flour and salt in a large bowl. Gradually add the shortening, tossing gently until all pieces are coated with flour. With a pastry blender or 2 knives, cut in shortening until mixture resembles coarse crumbs. Mix in the cheese. Sprinkle with ice water, 1 tablespoon at a time, tossing vigorously with a fork until the pastry just begins to hold together. Shape pastry into a ball, kneading lightly if necessary. Divide pastry into 2 balls, 1 slightly larger than the other. Flatten into 2 thick disks.

2 Preheat oven to 450°F. For filling, combine apples and lemon juice in a large bowl. Stir in the syrup. Add the brown sugar, flour, and cinnamon, tossing to coat.

3 On a lightly floured surface with a floured rolling pin, roll the larger disk into a 12-inch circle and fit into a 10-inch deep-dish pie pan, leaving a 1-inch overhang. Spoon apple mixture into pastry shell. Roll remaining pastry into an 11-inch circle. Cut vents and place on top of filling. Trim and flute edge of pastry.

4 Bake the pie for 10 minutes. Reduce oven temperature to 375°F. Bake for 50 to 60 minutes more or until apples are tender and filling is bubbly. (If pastry browns too quickly, cover top loosely with foil.) Cool pie completely on wire rack or serve warm. Makes 10 servings.

PER SERVING		DAILY GOAL
Calories	410	2,000 (F), 2,500 (M)
Total fat	18 g	60 g or less (F), 70 g or less (M)
Saturated fat	6 g	20 g or less (F), 23 g or less (M)
Cholesterol	12 mg	300 mg or less
Sodium	184 mg	2,400 mg or less
Carbohydrates	58 g	250 g or more
Protein	6 g	55 g to 90 g

MOLASSES-SPICE APPLE PIE

Prep time: 25 minutes plus chilling
Baking time: 75 minutes
● *Degree of difficulty: moderate*

Double Flaky Pastry (recipe, page 8)
- ⅔ cup firmly packed brown sugar
- 2 tablespoons all-purpose flour
- ½ teaspoon cinnamon
- ¼ teaspoon ginger
- 8 cups peeled, sliced Golden Delicious apples (7 *or* 8)
- ¼ cup light molasses
- 1 tablespoon butter, cut up

1 Prepare Double Flaky Pastry as directed, except chill pastry disks for 30 minutes.

2 Preheat oven to 425°F. For filling, combine brown sugar, flour, cinnamon, and ginger in a bowl. Add apples and toss to coat. Add the molasses and toss again.

3 On a lightly floured surface, roll the larger disk into a 12-inch circle and fit into a 9-inch pie pan, leaving a 1-inch overhang. Spoon apple mixture into pastry shell. Dot with butter. Roll remaining pastry into an 11-inch circle. Cut vents and place on top of filling. Trim and flute edge.

4 Place the pie on a cookie sheet and bake 15 minutes. Reduce oven temperature to 375°F. Bake for 60 minutes more or until the apples are tender and filling is bubbly. (If pastry browns too quickly, cover top loosely with foil.) Cool pie on a wire rack 1 hour. Makes 8 servings.

PER SERVING		DAILY GOAL
Calories	485	2,000 (F), 2,500 (M)
Total fat	20 g	60 g or less (F), 70 g or less (M)
Saturated fat	10 g	20 g or less (F), 23 g or less (M)
Cholesterol	35 mg	300 mg or less
Sodium	280 mg	2,400 mg or less
Carbohydrates	75 g	250 g or more
Protein	4 g	55 g to 90 g

BIG MAC APPLE PIE

Here's a tribute to our favorite eating apple—the McIntosh!

Prep time: 25 minutes plus chilling
Baking time: 50 minutes
Degree of difficulty: moderate

Double Flaky Pastry *or* Old-Fashioned Vinegar Pastry (recipes, page 8)
¾ **cup granulated sugar**
¼ **cup firmly packed brown sugar**
3 **tablespoons all-purpose flour**
1 **teaspoon cinnamon**
⅛ **teaspoon nutmeg**
6 **cups peeled, thinly sliced McIntosh apples (5 *or* 6)**
¼ **cup light corn syrup**
2 **tablespoons butter, cut up**
1 **tablespoon heavy *or* whipping cream**
Granulated sugar

1 Prepare Double Flaky Pastry or Old-Fashioned Vinegar Pastry as directed.

2 Preheat oven to 425°F. For filling, combine the ¾ cup granulated sugar, brown sugar, flour, cinnamon, and nutmeg in a large bowl. Add the apples and corn syrup and toss to blend. Set aside.

3 On a lightly floured surface with a floured rolling pin, roll the larger disk into a 12-inch circle and fit into a 9-inch pie pan, leaving a 1-inch overhang. Spoon apple mixture into pastry shell. Dot with butter. Roll remaining pastry into an 11-inch circle. Cut vents and place on top of filling. Trim and flute edge. Brush pastry with cream and sprinkle with sugar.

4 Bake pie 20 minutes. Reduce oven temperature to 350°F. Bake 30 minutes more or until apples are tender and filling is bubbly. (If pastry browns too quickly, cover top loosely with foil.) Cool on a wire rack. Makes 8 servings.

PER SERVING		DAILY GOAL
Calories	495	2,000 (F), 2,500 (M)
Total fat	22 g	60 g or less (F), 70 g or less (M)
Saturated fat	6 g	20 g or less (F), 23 g or less (M)
Cholesterol	10 mg	300 mg or less
Sodium	300 mg	2,400 mg or less
Carbohydrates	73 g	250 g or more
Protein	4 g	55 g to 90 g

MOM'S CLASSIC APPLE PIE

Everyone's favorite—a double crust apple pie fresh from the oven, bubbling with sweet heavy cream. We love this pie prepared with our super flaky Old-Fashioned Vinegar Pastry. *Also pictured on page 10.*

Prep time: 35 minutes plus chilling
Baking time: 70 to 75 minutes
● *Degree of difficulty: moderate*

Old-Fashioned Vinegar Pastry (recipe, page 8)
½ **cup granulated sugar**
3 **tablespoons all-purpose flour**
1 **teaspoon cinnamon**
⅛ **teaspoon nutmeg**
⅛ **teaspoon salt**
3 **pounds tart apples (Granny Smith, Jonathan *or* Pippin), peeled, cored, and cut into ¾-inch wedges (6 *or* 7)**
2 **teaspoons fresh lemon juice**
2 **tablespoons butter *or* margarine, cut up**
½ **cup heavy *or* whipping cream**

1 Prepare Old-Fashioned Vinegar Pastry as directed.

2 Preheat oven to 425°F. For filling, combine the sugar, flour, cinnamon, nutmeg, and salt in a large bowl. Add the apples and lemon juice, tossing well to blend. Set aside.

3 On a lightly floured surface with a floured rolling pin, roll the larger disk into a 12-inch circle and fit into a 9-inch pie pan, leaving a 1-inch overhang. Spoon the apple mixture into the pastry shell. Dot with butter.

4 Roll the remaining pastry into an 11-inch circle. Cut into ten 1-inch-wide strips and arrange in a lattice pattern on top of apples. Trim the lattice ends. Fold pastry over lattice ends and flute edge of pastry.

5 Place the pie on a cookie sheet and bake for 15 minutes. Reduce oven temperature to 375°F. Bake for 45 to 50 minutes more or until apples are tender. Pour the cream evenly over the exposed filling. Bake for 10 minutes more or until filling is bubbly and crust is golden. Cool pie completely on a wire rack or serve warm. Makes 8 servings.

PER SERVING		DAILY GOAL
Calories	480	2,000 (F), 2,500 (M)
Total fat	25 g	60 g or less (F), 70 g or less (M)
Saturated fat	14 g	20 g or less (F), 23 g or less (M)
Cholesterol	59 mg	300 mg or less
Sodium	324 mg	2,400 mg or less
Carbohydrates	61 g	250 g or more
Protein	4 g	55 g to 90 g

NOTES

VICE-PRESIDENT ALBERT GORE JR.'S APPLE PIE

This was a prize-winning entry from our star-spangled apple pie contest in 1988. Submitted by the Vice President's mother, the pie features apples flavored with orange juice and nutmeg under a lattice top.

Prep time: 40 minutes plus chilling
Baking time: 65 to 75 minutes
● *Degree of difficulty: moderate*

Double Flaky Pastry
  (recipe, page 8)
1   **cup granulated sugar**
¾   **cup orange juice**
¼   **cup butter *or* margarine**
1   **tablespoon all-purpose flour**
½   **teaspoon nutmeg**
3   **medium Winesap *or* Rome Beauty apples, peeled, cored, and thinly sliced**

1   Prepare the Double Flaky Pastry as directed.

2   Preheat oven to 400°F. For filling, combine the sugar, orange juice, butter, flour, and nutmeg in a small saucepan. Cook, stirring, over low heat until the sugar is dissolved and butter is melted.

3   On a lightly floured surface with a floured rolling pin, roll the larger disk into a 12-inch circle and fit into a 9-inch pie pan, leaving a 1-inch overhang. Spoon the apples into the pastry. Pour the sugar-orange mixture over apples.

4   Roll the remaining pastry into an 11-inch circle. Cut into ten 1-inch-wide strips and arrange in a lattice pattern on top of apples. Trim lattice ends. Fold bottom pastry over lattice ends and flute edge.

5   Bake for 15 minutes. Reduce oven temperature to 350°F. Bake for 50 to 60 minutes more or until the apples are tender. Cool pie completely on a wire rack or serve warm. Makes 8 servings.

PER SERVING		DAILY GOAL
Calories	460	2,000 (F), 2,500 (M)
Total fat	24 g	60 g or less (F), 70 g or less (M)
Saturated fat	12 g	20 g or less (F), 23 g or less (M)
Cholesterol	46 mg	300 mg or less
Sodium 313	mg	2,400 mg or less
Carbohydrates	59 g	250 g or more
Protein	4 g	55 g to 90 g

NOTES

_____

_____

_____

_____

_____

_____

_____

_____

_____

_____

_____

_____

_____

_____

_____

APPLE-CRANBERRY TURNOVERS

Here's a lovely addition to the holiday dessert table. The apple-cranberry filling is a delightful surprise in these turnovers prepared with puff pastry.

Prep time: 1 hour plus chilling
Baking time: 20 minutes
O *Degree of difficulty: easy*

1 **package (17¼ ounces) frozen puff pastry, thawed**
2 **tablespoons butter *or* margarine**
3 **cups peeled, diced Golden Delicious apples (2 *or* 3)**
1 **cup fresh *or* frozen cranberries**
½ **cup granulated sugar**
¼ **teaspoon cinnamon**
¼ **teaspoon grated lemon peel**
1 **large egg**
 Pinch salt
½ **cup heavy *or* whipping cream**
 Confectioners' sugar

1 Cut the puff pastry into eight 4½-inch squares. Cover and refrigerate.

2 Melt the butter in a large skillet over medium heat. Add the apples and cranberries; cover and cook, stirring occasionally, about 10 minutes or until fruit is tender. Stir in the sugar and cook for 1 minute more, stirring to break up apples. Stir in the cinnamon and lemon peel. Transfer the fruit mixture to a medium bowl and cool.

3 Place a pastry square on a work surface. Brush edges lightly with water. Place 1 rounded tablespoon of the fruit mixture in the center and fold pastry in half to form a triangle. Place on a cookie sheet. Repeat with remaining pastry and 7 more tablespoons fruit mixture. (Reserve remaining fruit mixture.) Beat together the egg and salt in a cup. Press edges of turnovers with tines of a fork, then brush with beaten egg. Cover and refrigerate 30 minutes.

4 Preheat oven to 400°F. Brush the turnovers again with egg. Bake for 20 minutes or until golden. Transfer turnovers to a wire rack and cool completely.

5 Meanwhile, beat the cream in a small mixing bowl until soft peaks form. Fold in reserved fruit mixture. Sprinkle turnovers with confectioners' sugar and serve fruited cream on the side. Makes 8 servings.

PER SERVING		DAILY GOAL
Calories	505	2,000 (F), 2,500 (M)
Total fat	32 g	60 g or less (F), 70 g or less (M)
Saturated fat	9 g	20 g or less (F), 23 g or less (M)
Cholesterol	55 mg	300 mg or less
Sodium	212 mg	2,400 mg or less
Carbohydrates	50 g	250 g or more
Protein	6 g	55 g to 90 g

NOTES

17

CRANBERRY-APPLE PIE

Apples and cranberries make a beautiful combination, both to the eye and the palate. The addition of cream during the final few minutes of baking gives the tart fruit filling extra smoothness.

Prep time: 25 to 30 minutes plus
chilling
Baking time: 70 minutes
Degree of difficulty: moderate

Double Flaky Pastry *or* Old-Fashioned Vinegar Pastry (recipes, page 8)
¾ **cup firmly packed brown sugar**
¼ **cup granulated sugar**
⅓ **cup all-purpose flour**
1 **teaspoon cinnamon**
4 **cups peeled, sliced, tart apples (Granny Smith, Jonathan *or* Pippin) (3 *or* 4)**
2 **cups chopped fresh *or* frozen cranberries**
2 **tablespoons butter, cut up**
½ **cup heavy *or* whipping cream**

1 Prepare Double Flaky Pastry or Old-Fashioned Vinegar Pastry as directed.

2 For filling, combine the brown sugar, granulated sugar, flour, and cinnamon in a large bowl. Add the apples and cranberries, tossing to coat.

3 Preheat oven to 425°F. On a lightly floured surface with a floured rolling pin, roll the larger disk into a 12-inch circle and fit into a 9-inch pie pan, leaving a 1-inch overhang. Spoon the apple-cranberry mixture into the pastry shell. Dot with butter. Brush overhang with water.

4 Roll remaining pastry into an 11-inch circle. Cut vents and place on top of filling. Trim and flute edge of pastry.

5 Bake pie for 15 minutes. Reduce oven temperature to 350°F. Bake for 50 minutes more or until the apples are tender and filling is bubbly. (If pastry browns too quickly, cover top loosely with foil.) With a small sharp knife, re-cut vents and pour cream through vents. Bake 5 minutes more. Cool pie completely on a wire rack or serve warm. Makes 8 servings.

PER SERVING		DAILY GOAL
Calories	575	2,000 (F), 2,500 (M)
Total fat	33 g	60 g or less (F), 70 g or less (M)
Saturated fat	11 g	20 g or less (F), 23 g or less (M)
Cholesterol	55 mg	300 mg or less
Sodium	603 mg	2,400 mg or less
Carbohydrates	68 g	250 g or more
Protein	5 g	55 g to 90 g

NOTES

_____
_____
_____
_____
_____
_____
_____
_____
_____
_____
_____
_____
_____
_____

19

CLASSIC APPLE CRUMB PIE

Prep time: 20 minutes plus chilling
Baking time: 25 to 30 minutes
○ *Degree of difficulty: easy*

Single Flaky Pastry (recipe, page 7)

Topping
- 1 cup all-purpose flour
- ¾ cup firmly packed brown sugar
- ¼ cup butter, melted

Filling
- ½ cup granulated sugar
- ¼ teaspoon cinnamon
- ⅛ teaspoon nutmeg
- 4 cups peeled and diced tart apples (Granny Smith, Jonathan, *or* Pippin) (3 *or* 4)
- 1½ teaspoons butter, cut up

1 Prepare Single Flaky Pastry as directed.

2 For topping, combine the flour and brown sugar in a medium bowl. Stir in the butter until mixture is evenly moistened and crumbly. Set aside.

3 Preheat oven to 425°F. For filling, combine the sugar, cinnamon, and nutmeg in a small bowl. Spoon the apples into pastry shell. Sprinkle apples with sugar and spice mixture and dot with butter.

4 Pat topping evenly over apples. Bake 10 minutes. Reduce oven temperature to 375°F. Bake 25 to 30 minutes more or until apples are tender. (If topping browns too quickly, cover loosely with foil.) Cool pie on a wire rack. Makes 8 servings.

PER SERVING		DAILY GOAL
Calories	460	2,000 (F), 2,500 (M)
Total fat	18 g	60 g or less (F), 70 g or less (M)
Saturated fat	10 g	20 g or less (F), 23 g or less (M)
Cholesterol	41 mg	300 mg or less
Sodium	140 mg	2,400 mg or less
Carbohydrates	70 g	250 g or more
Protein	4 g	55 g to 90 g

DUTCH APPLE CUSTARD PIE

This spicy Dutch apple pie from the Meadow View Farm Market in Kutztown, Pennsylvania, boasts a nutty whole wheat crust.

Prep time: 25 minutes plus chilling
Baking time: 50 minutes
○ *Degree of difficulty: easy*

Whole Wheat Pastry
- 1 cup all-purpose flour
- 2 tablespoons whole wheat flour
- ½ teaspoon baking powder
- ¼ cup vegetable shortening
- 4 to 5 tablespoons ice water

Custard Filling
- ¾ cup firmly packed brown sugar
- 3 tablespoons all-purpose flour
- ¼ teaspoon cinnamon
- 1 large egg
- 1 cup heavy *or* whipping cream
- 1 tablespoon butter *or* margarine, melted
- 1 teaspoon vanilla extract
- 3 cups peeled, thinly sliced, tart apples (Granny Smith, Jonathan, *or* Pippin)

1 For Whole Wheat Pastry, combine the all-purpose and whole wheat flours and baking powder in a medium bowl. Gradually add the shortening, tossing gently until all pieces are coated with flour. With a pastry blender or 2 knives, cut in shortening until mixture resembles coarse crumbs. Add ice water, 1 tablespoon at a time, tossing vigorously with a fork until pastry just begins to hold together. On a smooth surface, shape the pastry into a ball, kneading lightly if necessary; flatten into a thick disk. Wrap tightly in plastic wrap and refrigerate 1 hour.

2 Preheat oven to 425°F. For Custard Filling, combine the brown sugar, flour, and cinnamon in a large bowl. Whisk in the egg, cream, butter, and vanilla until blended. Add the apples, tossing to coat.

3 On a lightly floured surface with a floured rolling pin, roll pastry into a 12-inch circle and fit into a 9-inch pie pan, leaving a 1-inch overhang. Trim and flute. Spoon filling into pastry shell. Bake 10 minutes. Reduce oven temperature to 350°F. Bake for 40 minutes more or until custard is set in center. Cool pie on a wire rack. Makes 8 servings.

PER SERVING		DAILY GOAL
Calories	360	2,000 (F), 2,500 (M)
Total fat	20 g	60 g or less (F), 70 g or less (M)
Saturated fat	10 g	20 g or less (F), 23 g or less (M)
Cholesterol	71 mg	300 mg or less
Sodium	67 mg	2,400 mg or less
Carbohydrates	43 g	250 g or more
Protein	4 g	55 g to 90 g

AN APPLE A DAY

Remember to always store apples in the refrigerator to maintain their crisp texture. A plastic or paper bag will help retain their moisture.

The following varieties of apples are especially suited for baking:

Granny Smith: Available year round, this is the tastiest all-purpose apple for baking. Bright green, juicy, crisp, and very firm. Good for eating and cooking and blends well with other varieties.

Pippin: Available September through the spring. Bright green, firm, and mildly tart. This is an excellent pie apple.

Baldwin: Available October through April. Flecked red and yellow skin and mildly tart.

Gravenstein: Available August to late September. Sweetly tart, juicy, and crisp. Green skin streaked with red.

Jonathan: Available September through the spring. This all-purpose apple is yellow or green with pale to bright red stripes. It has a moderately tart flavor, and is crisp and rich.

Cortland: Available September through early spring. Deep red and juicy with an assertive fruitiness.

Golden Delicious: Available September through early summer. This variety holds it's shape well in cooking. Rich yellow, juicy, and tangy.

McIntosh: Available September through late spring. Mixed red and green blush. Juicy with a sweet-tart flavor.

Rome Beauty: Available October to early summer. This is an excellent apple for baking and cooking. Red striped to solid red. Sweet and mellow flavor.

Winesap: Available November through May. Slightly tart with a deep red skin.

SENATOR ROBERT DOLE'S APPLE PIE

This 1988 Ladies' Home Journal first prize apple pie winner was from the senator's wife, Elizabeth Dole. The press-in-the-pan pastry is speckled with pecans, filled with gently cooked apples, and topped with a nut-sugar streusel.

Prep time: 35 minutes plus chilling
Baking time: 40 minutes
● *Degree of difficulty: moderate*

Filling
- 6 tart apples (Granny Smith, Jonathan, *or* Pippin), peeled, cored, and sliced
- ⅔ cup granulated sugar
- Water
- 2 tablespoons cornstarch
- 1 tablespoon butter
- ½ teaspoon cinnamon
- Pinch nutmeg

Pastry
- ½ cup butter, softened
- ⅓ cup firmly packed brown sugar
- 1¼ cups all-purpose flour
- ½ cup chopped pecans

Topping
- ½ cup all-purpose flour
- ½ cup chopped pecans
- ¼ cup firmly packed brown sugar
- ½ teaspoon cinnamon
- ¼ teaspoon ginger
- ⅛ teaspoon mace
- ¼ cup cold butter, cut up

1 For filling, combine the apples, sugar, and ½ cup water in a large skillet. Bring to a simmer over medium heat, then cover and cook 5 minutes. Dissolve the cornstarch in ¼ cup water in a small bowl; stir into apple mixture. Bring to a boil, then cook, stirring occasionally, 2 minutes. Remove from heat. Stir in the butter, cinnamon, and nutmeg. Cool.

2 For pastry, beat the butter and brown sugar in a mixing bowl with an electric mixer on medium speed until light and fluffy. With mixer at low speed, beat in the flour and pecans. Press dough into a 10-inch pie plate and refrigerate 10 minutes.

3 Meanwhile, for the topping, combine the flour, pecans, brown sugar, cinnamon, ginger, and mace in a medium bowl. With a pastry blender or 2 knives, cut in the butter until mixture resembles coarse crumbs. Set aside.

4 Spoon the filling into the pastry shell. Sprinkle topping evenly over apples. Bake for 10 minutes. Reduce oven temperature to 375°F. Bake for 30 minutes more or until apples are tender. (If topping browns too quickly, cover loosely with foil.) Cool on a wire rack. Makes 8 servings.

PER SERVING		DAILY GOAL
Calories	550	2,000 (F), 2,500 (M)
Total fat	28 g	60 g or less (F), 70 g or less (M)
Saturated fat	12 g	20 g or less (F), 23 g or less (M)
Cholesterol	50 mg	300 mg or less
Sodium	196 mg	2,400 mg or less
Carbohydrates	74 g	250 g or more
Protein	4 g	55 g to 90 g

NOTES

GOLDEN PARMESAN APPLE PIE

Any tart green apple is perfect in this pie, but be sure to use freshly grated Parmesan cheese in the buttery crumb topping.

Prep time: 40 minutes plus chilling
Baking time: 65 to 70 minutes
○ *Degree of difficulty: easy*

Single Flaky Pastry (recipe, page 7)

Topping
¾ **cup firmly packed brown sugar**
¾ **cup all-purpose flour**
½ **cup freshly grated Parmesan cheese**
6 **tablespoons cold butter** *or* **margarine, cut up**

Filling
½ **cup firmly packed brown sugar**
¼ **cup granulated sugar**
3 **tablespoons all-purpose flour**
1 **teaspoon cinnamon**
¼ **teaspoon nutmeg**
¼ **teaspoon salt**

3 **pounds tart apples (Granny Smith, Jonathan,** *or* **Pippin), peeled, cored and sliced ½-inch thick**

1 Prepare Single Flaky Pastry as directed and chill for 1 hour. On a lightly floured surface with a floured rolling pin, roll the pastry into a 13-inch circle and fit into a 10-inch pie pan, letting pastry overhang edge. Trim and flute edge of pastry. Freeze for 15 minutes.

2 For topping, combine the brown sugar, flour, and Parmesan cheese in a medium bowl. With a pastry blender or 2 knives, cut in the butter until mixture resembles coarse crumbs. Set aside.

3 Preheat oven to 450°F. For filling, combine the brown sugar, granulated sugar, flour, cinnamon, nutmeg, and salt in a large bowl. Add the apples, tossing until well coated. Spoon filling into pastry shell and sprinkle on topping.

4 Bake 10 minutes. Reduce oven temperature to 375°F. Bake 55 to 60 minutes more or until filling is bubbly and apples are tender. (If topping browns too quickly, cover loosely with foil.) Cool on a wire rack or serve warm. Makes 8 servings.

PER SERVING		DAILY GOAL	
Calories	585	2,000 (F), 2,500 (M)	
Total fat	23 g	60 g or less (F), 70 g or less (M)	
Saturated fat	13 g	20 g or less (F), 23 g or less (M)	
Cholesterol	51 mg	300 mg or less	
Sodium	438 mg	2,400 mg or less	
Carbohydrates	91 g	250 g or more	
Protein	7 g	55 g to 90 g	

NOTES

SOUR CREAM APPLE PIE

This creamy apple pie with a crunchy streusel topping is adapted from the book *Quiche and Pie*, by Irena Chalmers, Susan Wright, and Gladys McConnell. For pure indulgence, slice it while it's warm and serve it with a drizzle of heavy cream.

Prep time: 30 minutes plus chilling
Baking time: 1 hour
⬤ *Degree of difficulty: moderate*

Single Flaky Pastry (recipe, page 7)

Topping
- ½ **cup granulated sugar**
- ½ **cup all-purpose flour**
- 1 **teaspoon cinnamon**
- ½ **cup cold butter, cut up**
  (no substitutions)

Filling
- 1 **cup sour cream**
- 1 **large egg, lightly beaten**
- 2 **tablespoons flour**
- 2 **teaspoons fresh lemon juice**

- 3 **cups peeled, sliced, tart apples (Granny Smith, Jonathan *or* Pippin) (2 *or* 3)**
  Heavy *or* whipping cream (optional)

1 Prepare Single Flaky Pastry as directed.

2 Preheat oven to 400°F. Line pastry shell with foil and fill with dried beans or uncooked rice. Bake for 7 minutes. Remove foil and beans. Bake pastry for 5 minutes more. Cool on a wire rack.

3 Meanwhile, for topping, combine the sugar, flour, and cinnamon in a medium bowl. With a pastry blender or 2 knives, cut in the butter until mixture resembles coarse crumbs. Set aside.

4 Reduce oven temperature to 375°F. For filling, combine the sour cream, egg, flour, and lemon juice in a medium bowl. Fold in the apples. Spoon the filling into the baked crust, then sprinkle with topping. Bake about 1 hour or until filling is bubbly and topping is golden. Serve warm with cream. Makes 8 servings.

PER SERVING WITHOUT CREAM		DAILY GOAL
Calories	470	2,000 (F), 2,500 (M)
Total fat	30 g	60 g or less (F), 70 g or less (M)
Saturated fat	17 g	20 g or less (F), 23 g or less (M)
Cholesterol	94 mg	300 mg or less
Sodium	296 mg	2,400 mg or less
Carbohydrates	45 g	250 g or more
Protein	5 g	55 g to 90 g

NOTES

TWIN HILL RANCH FRENCH APPLE PIE

Here's a fabulous crumb-topped pie from the Twin Hill apple ranch in Sebastopol, California. From over a hundred pies baked a day, it's the biggest seller, made from the Fuji variety of apple grown on the ranch.

Prep time: 35 minutes plus chilling
Baking time: 65 to 70 minutes
● *Degree of difficulty: moderate*

Crust
- 1 **cup all-purpose flour**
- ¾ **teaspoon granulated sugar**
- ¼ **teaspoon baking powder**
- ¼ **teaspoon salt**
- ¼ **cup cold butter, cut up (no substitutions)**
- 3 **tablespoons vegetable shortening**
- 1 **teaspoon distilled white vinegar**
- 2 **to 3 tablespoons ice water**

French Topping
- ½ **cup granulated sugar**
- ½ **cup old-fashioned oats, uncooked**
- ¼ **cup all-purpose flour**
- ½ **teaspoon baking powder**
- ¼ **teaspoon cinnamon**
- ¼ **teaspoon ground ginger**
- ⅛ **teaspoon mace**
- ½ **cup cold butter, cut up (no substitutions)**

Filling
- ½ **cup granulated sugar**
- 1 **teaspoon cinnamon**
- 3 **pounds baking apples, peeled, cored, and thinly sliced**

1 For crust, combine the flour, sugar, baking powder, and salt in a medium bowl. Gradually add the butter and shortening, tossing gently until all pieces are coated with flour. With a pastry blender or 2 knives, cut in the butter and shortening until mixture resembles coarse crumbs. Sprinkle with the vinegar then add ice water, 1 tablespoon at a time, tossing vigorously with a fork until pastry just begins to hold together. On a smooth surface, shape pastry into a ball, kneading lightly if necessary. Flatten into a thick disk. Wrap tightly in plastic wrap and refrigerate 1 hour or overnight.

2 For French Topping, combine the sugar, oats, flour, baking powder, cinnamon, ginger, and mace in a medium bowl. With a pastry blender or 2 knives, cut in the butter until mixture resembles coarse crumbs. Set aside.

3 Preheat oven to 400°F. On a floured surface, roll pastry into a 12-inch circle. Fit into a 9-inch pie plate. Trim and flute edge of pastry.

4 For filling, combine the sugar and cinnamon in a large bowl. Add the apples, tossing to coat. Spoon filling into prepared pie shell. Sprinkle topping evenly over apples. Bake for 15 minutes. Reduce oven temperature to 375°F. Bake for 50 to 55 minutes more or until apples are tender. (If topping browns too quickly, cover loosely with foil.) Cool pie on a wire rack. Makes 8 servings.

PER SERVING		DAILY GOAL	
Calories	425	2,000 (F), 2,500 (M)	
Total fat	18 g	60 g or less (F), 70 g or less (M)	
Saturated fat	11 g	20 g or less (F), 23 g or less (M)	
Cholesterol	47 mg	300 mg or less	
Sodium	284 mg	2,400 mg or less	
Carbohydrates	65 g	250 g or more	
Protein	3 g	55 g to 90 g	

THE BEST OF

SUMMER'S PIES

Here's a peach of a deal—a great collection of warm weather fruit pies, bursting with the best tastes of the season. We've got golden sweet peaches, wrapped in phyllo or paired with huckleberries. Berries stand alone in our Blackberry Custard Pie, Fresh Raspberry Pie, and Big and Beautiful Blueberry Pie. Or, choose a different twist on your summer fruit pie with Plum-Orange Lattice Pie. There's simply no better way to celebrate the fruits of summer than with a piece of pie.

BIG AND BEAUTIFUL BLUEBERRY PIE

Bubbly and gorgeous, this pie is summer's best. The filling can be prepared with either fresh or unthawed frozen blueberries.

Prep time: 25 minutes plus chilling
Baking time: 70 minutes
● *Degree of difficulty: moderate*

Double Flaky Pastry *or* Old-Fashioned Vinegar Pastry (recipes, page 8)
5 **cups fresh blueberries**
⅔ **cup plus 1 teaspoon granulated sugar, divided**
¼ **cup all-purpose flour**
1 **teaspoon grated lemon peel**
¼ **teaspoon cinnamon**
  Pinch cloves
2 **tablespoons fresh lemon juice**
1 **tablespoon butter *or* margarine**
2 **teaspoons milk**

1 Prepare Double Flaky Pastry or Old-Fashioned Vinegar Pastry as directed.

2 Place a cookie sheet on the middle rack of oven. Preheat oven to 450°F. For filling, combine the blueberries, ⅔ cup of the sugar, flour, lemon peel, cinnamon, and cloves in a large bowl, tossing well to coat berries. Set aside.

3 On a lightly floured surface with a floured rolling pin, roll the larger disk into a 12-inch circle and fit into a 9-inch pie pan, leaving a 1-inch overhang. Spoon blueberry mixture into pastry shell. Drizzle with lemon juice and dot with butter. Roll remaining pastry into a 10-inch circle and place on top of filling. With a small sharp knife, cut vents in top pastry for steam to escape. Trim and flute edge of pastry. Brush pastry with milk and sprinkle with the remaining 1 teaspoon sugar.

4 Place pie on cookie sheet and bake for 20 minutes. Reduce oven temperature to 375°F. Bake for 50 minutes more or until filling is bubbly in center. (If pastry browns too quickly, cover top loosely with foil.) Cool pie on a wire rack at least 1 hour before serving. Makes 8 servings.

PER SERVING		DAILY GOAL
Calories	420	2,000 (F), 2,500 (M)
Total fat	20 g	60 g or less (F), 70 g or less (M)
Saturated fat	10 g	20 g or less (F), 23 g or less (M)
Cholesterol	35 mg	300 mg or less
Sodium	275 mg	2,400 mg or less
Carbohydrates	57 g	250 g or more
Protein	4 g	55 g to 90 g

BUBBLY FRUIT PIES

For many of our fruit pies, the fillings are extra-generous. To catch all the drips, preheat the oven as directed and adjust the oven rack to the center position. When your pie is ready to bake, place it on a cookie sheet and bake as directed.

DEEP-DISH PEACH PIE

Because summer peaches are so juicy, we skipped the bottom pastry for this pie. What's left? Succulent peach filling crowned by a flaky crust.

Prep time: 30 minutes plus chilling
Baking time: 45 to 60 minutes
O *Degree of difficulty: easy*

Pastry

1 **cup all-purpose flour**
¼ **teaspoon salt**
¼ **cup cold butter** *or* **margarine, cut up**
1 **tablespoon vegetable shortening**
1 **to 2 tablespoons ice water**

Filling

⅔ **cup plus 2 tablespoons granulated sugar, divided**
¼ **cup all-purpose flour**
¼ **teaspoon grated lemon peel**
3 **pounds ripe peaches, peeled and sliced (6 cups)**
2 **teaspoons fresh lemon juice**
1 **teaspoon vanilla extract**
1 **tablespoon butter** *or* **margarine, cut up**

1 **tablespoon milk**
   Vanilla ice cream

1 For pastry, combine the flour and salt in a medium bowl. Gradually add the butter and shortening, tossing gently until all pieces are coated with flour. With a pastry blender or 2 knives, cut in butter and shortening until mixture resembles coarse crumbs. Sprinkle with water, 1 tablespoon at a time, tossing vigorously with a fork until pastry just begins to hold together. On a smooth surface, shape pastry into a ball, kneading lightly if necessary. Flatten into a thick disk. Wrap tightly in plastic wrap and refrigerate at least 30 minutes.

2 Preheat oven to 425°F. For filling, combine ⅔ cup of the sugar, flour, and lemon peel in a large bowl. Add the peaches, lemon juice, and vanilla, tossing to combine. Spoon mixture into a 10-inch deep-dish pie plate and dot with butter.

3 On a lightly floured surface with a floured rolling pin, roll pastry to an 11-inch circle. Cut decorative vents. Place pastry on top of peaches and flute edges. Or, cut pastry into ½-inch-wide strips and arrange on top of pie to form a lattice. Brush pastry with milk and sprinkle with the remaining 2 tablespoons sugar.

4 Place pie on a cookie sheet and bake for 15 minutes. Reduce oven temperature to 375°F. Bake for 30 to 45 minutes more or until filling is bubbly in center. Cool on wire rack for 20 minutes. Serve with vanilla ice cream. Makes 8 servings.

PER SERVING		DAILY GOAL
Calories	285	2,000 (F), 2,500 (M)
Total fat	9 g	60 g or less (F), 70 g or less (M)
Saturated fat	5 g	20 g or less (F), 23 g or less (M)
Cholesterol	20 mg	300 mg or less
Sodium	142 mg	2,400 mg or less
Carbohydrates	49 g	250 g or more
Protein	3 g	55 g to 90 g

NOTES

JUMBLE BERRY PIE

This is pure summertime heaven: a mix of peak season berries baked together under a lattice crust.

Prep time: 20 minutes
Baking time: 65 to 75 minutes
Degree of difficulty: easy

Double Flaky Pastry *or* Old-Fashioned Vinegar Pastry (recipes, page 8)
¾ **cup plus 1 tablespoon granulated sugar, divided**
¼ **cup all-purpose flour**
3 **cups fresh blueberries**
1½ **cups fresh raspberries**
1½ **cups fresh blackberries**
1 **tablespoon butter, cut up**
1 **tablespoon heavy cream *or* milk**

1 Prepare Double Flaky Pastry or Old-Fashioned Vinegar Pastry as directed.

2 Preheat oven to 425°F. For filling, combine ¾ cup of the sugar and the flour in a large bowl. Add the blueberries, raspberries, and blackberries, tossing to coat.

3 On a lightly floured surface with a floured rolling pin, roll the larger pastry disk into an 11-inch circle and fit into a 9-inch pie pan, leaving a 1-inch overhang. Spoon the berry mixture into the pastry shell and dot with butter.

4 Roll remaining pastry into a 9-inch circle. Cut into ½-inch-wide strips using a fluted pastry cutter and arrange in a lattice pattern on top of filling. Trim lattice ends. Fold bottom pastry over lattice ends and flute edge of pastry. Brush pastry with the cream then sprinkle with the remaining 1 tablespoon sugar.

5 Place pie on a cookie sheet and bake for 15 minutes. Reduce oven temperature to 375°F. and bake for 50 to 60 minutes more or until center is bubbly. Cool on a wire rack. Makes 8 servings.

PER SERVING		DAILY GOAL
Calories	440	2,000 (F), 2,500 (M)
Total fat	21 g	60 g or less (F), 70 g or less (M)
Saturated fat	10 g	20 g or less (F), 23 g or less (M)
Cholesterol	37 mg	300 mg or less
Sodium	273 mg	2,400 mg or less
Carbohydrates	61 g	250 g or more
Protein	5 g	55 g to 90 g

THE BERRY BEST PIES

Berries freeze beautifully for pie fillings. Simply arrange a supply of your favorite berries or pitted cherries about ½-inch apart on cookie sheets, then freeze until completely firm. Transfer the frozen berries to freezer-proof bags or containers. When ready to use, add the frozen berries, unthawed, to your pie filling and bake as directed.

NOTES

_____

_____

_____

_____

_____

_____

_____

_____

PLUM-ORANGE LATTICE PIE

Fresh orange juice and peel bring out the natural sweetness in the plums, making a perfect late summer fruit pie.

Prep time: 25 minutes
Baking time: 55 to 60 minutes
Degree of difficulty: moderate

Double Flaky Pastry
   (recipe, page 8)
1   **cup granulated sugar**
3   **tablespoons quick-cooking tapioca**
2   **tablespoons fresh orange juice**
½   **teaspoon vanilla extract**
¼   **teaspoon grated orange peel**
6   **cups sliced fresh plums**
1   **tablespoon butter *or* margarine, cut up**
1   **large egg, lightly beaten**

1   Prepare Double Flaky Pastry as directed.

2   For filling, combine the sugar, tapioca, orange juice, vanilla, and orange peel in a large bowl. Add the plums, gently tossing to coat. Let stand for 15 minutes.

3   Preheat oven to 450°F. On a lightly floured surface with a floured rolling pin, roll the larger disk into a 12-inch circle and fit into a 9-inch pie pan, leaving a 1-inch overhang. Spoon plum mixture into pastry shell. Dot with butter.

4   Roll remaining pastry into a 10-inch circle. Cut into ten 1-inch-wide strips and arrange in a lattice pattern on top of filling. Trim lattice ends. Fold bottom pastry over lattice ends and flute edge of pastry. Brush pastry with beaten egg.

5   Place pie on a cookie sheet and bake for 20 minutes. Reduce oven temperature to 375°F. Bake for 35 to 40 minutes more or until filling is bubbly and crust is golden. Cool pie on a wire rack at least 1 hour before serving. Makes 8 servings.

PER SERVING		DAILY GOAL
Calories	460	2,000 (F), 2,500 (M)
Total fat	19 g	60 g or less (F), 70 g or less (M)
Saturated fat	10 g	20 g or less (F), 23 g or less (M)
Cholesterol	61 mg	300 mg or less
Sodium	294 mg	2,400 mg or less
Carbohydrates	69 g	250 g or more
Protein	5 g	55 g to 90 g

SOUR CHERRY PIE

Tart cherries are available from late June through July and they're quite perishable, so refrigerate them and use them within a day or two. Be sure to wash the fruit just before using and discard any shriveled or mushy fruit.

Prep time: 25 minutes plus chilling
Baking time: 60 to 70 minutes
Degree of difficulty: moderate

Double Flaky Pastry *or* Old-Fashioned Vinegar Pastry (recipes, page 8)
1   **cup plus 1 tablespoon granulated sugar, divided**
3   **tablespoons cornstarch**
⅛   **teaspoon cinnamon**
   Pinch salt
5   **cups fresh, pitted sour cherries, 1½ pounds frozen cherries, *or* 2 cans (16 ounces each) pitted sour cherries***
2   **tablespoons fresh lemon juice**
1   **tablespoon butter *or* margarine, cut up**

1 Prepare Double Flaky Pastry or Old-Fashioned Vinegar Pastry as directed.

2 Preheat oven to 425°F. On a lightly floured surface with a floured rolling pin, roll the larger disk into a 12-inch circle and fit into a 9-inch pie pan, leaving a 1-inch overhang.

3 For filling, combine 1 cup of the sugar, the cornstarch, cinnamon, and salt in a large bowl. Add the cherries and lemon juice, tossing gently to coat. Spoon cherry mixture into pastry shell. Dot with butter.

4 Between 2 sheets of wax paper, roll remaining pastry into a 10-inch circle. Cut into ½-inch-wide strips and arrange in a lattice pattern on top of cherries. Trim lattice ends. Fold bottom pastry over lattice ends and flute edge of pastry. Sprinkle lattice with the remaining 1 tablespoon sugar.

5 Place pie on cookie sheet and bake for 20 minutes. Reduce oven temperature to 375°F. Bake for 40 to 50 minutes more or until filling is bubbly in center. (If pastry browns too quickly, cover top loosely with foil.) Cool on wire rack at least 1 hour before serving. Makes 8 servings.

*For canned cherries: Drain the cherries, reserving ½ cup of their juice. Combine 1 cup granulated sugar, 3 tablespoons cornstarch, ⅛ teaspoon cinnamon, and a pinch of salt in a medium saucepan. Stir in the reserved cherry juice and 2 tablespoons fresh lemon juice. Bring to boil over medium heat, stirring constantly; boil 1 minute. Remove from heat and stir in cherries. Cool completely. Proceed with the recipe as directed.

PER SERVING		DAILY GOAL
Calories	430	2,000 (F), 2,500 (M)
Total fat	20 g	60 g or less (F), 70 g or less (M)
Saturated fat	10 g	20 g or less (F), 23 g or less (M)
Cholesterol	35 mg	300 mg or less
Sodium	288 mg	2,400 mg or less
Carbohydrates	61 g	250 g or more
Protein	4 g	55 g to 90 g

FREEZING FRUIT PIES

Freezing unbaked fruit pies preserves their freshest flavor. Prepare the fruit filling as usual, adding an extra tablespoon of thickener per pie. Finish the pie as directed, but for a double-crust pie, do not cut vents in the top crust. Wrap the pie well in freezer-proof wrap and freeze up to three months.

• To bake a frozen pie, preheat the oven. Unwrap the pie, place it on a cookie sheet and cut vents (if baking a double-crust pie). Bake the unthawed pie, adding 15 to 20 minutes to the baking time given in the recipe.

• To freeze a baked fruit pie, cool the pie completely and wrap it well in freezer-proof wrap. Freeze up to three months. Thaw at room temperature for 30 minutes. Unwrap the pie and bake it in a preheated 350°F. oven for 30 minutes.

BLUEBERRY-PEACH GALETTE

This free-form tart can be adapted to a 9-inch tart pan with a removable bottom. Roll pastry and fill as directed, but add 10 to 15 minutes to the baking time. To prevent overbrowning, cover pastry loosely with foil halfway through baking. *Also pictured on page 28.*

Prep time: *40 minutes*
Baking time: *50 minutes*
○ Degree of difficulty: *easy*

Pastry
1¼ **cups all-purpose flour**
  2 **teaspoons granulated sugar**
 ¾ **teaspoon salt**
  2 **tablespoons vegetable shortening**
  6 **tablespoons cold butter, cut up (no substitutions)**
  6 **to 7 tablespoons cold water**

Filling
  3 **pounds ripe peaches *or* nectarines, peeled and thinly sliced**
1¼ **cups fresh blueberries**

 ⅔ **cup plus ½ teaspoon granulated sugar, divided**
 ¼ **cup all-purpose flour**
  1 **tablespoon fresh lemon juice**
 ¼ **teaspoon cinnamon**
  1 **large egg white, lightly beaten**

1 Preheat oven to 400°F. For pastry, combine the flour, sugar, and salt in a medium bowl. With your fingers, work in shortening until mixture resembles cornmeal. With a pastry blender or 2 knives, cut in the butter until mixture resembles coarse crumbs. Add cold water, 1 tablespoon at a time, tossing vigorously with a fork until pastry just begins to hold together. On a smooth surface, shape pastry into a ball, kneading lightly if necessary. Set aside.

2 For filling, combine the peaches, blueberries, ⅔ cup of the sugar, flour, lemon juice, and cinnamon in a large bowl. Toss to coat well.

3 On a lightly floured surface with a floured rolling pin, roll pastry into an 18-inch circle. Fold into quarters, then unfold onto a large ungreased cookie sheet.

4 Spoon fruit filling in a mound in the center of pastry. Fold a 3-inch border of

pastry over fruit. Brush pastry lightly with egg white, then sprinkle with the remaining ½ teaspoon sugar.

5 Bake tart for 50 minutes or until center is bubbly. (If pastry browns too quickly, cover top loosely with foil.) Cool completely on a wire rack. Makes 10 servings.

PER SERVING		DAILY GOAL
Calories	265	2,000 (F), 2,500 (M)
Total fat	10 g	60 g or less (F), 70 g or less (M)
Saturated fat	5 g	20 g or less (F), 23 g or less (M)
Cholesterol	19 mg	300 mg or less
Sodium	242 mg	2,400 mg or less
Carbohydrates	43 g	250 g or more
Protein	3 g	55 g to 90 g

NOTES

_____

_____

_____

_____

_____

_____

_____

PEACH-HUCKLEBERRY PIE

We simply adored this late summer pie from the Wellen's Luscious Fruit and Antiques farm stand near Spokane, Washington. If fresh huckleberries aren't available in your area, simply substitute fresh blueberries.

Prep time: 1 hour plus chilling
Baking time: 50 to 55 minutes
Degree of difficulty: moderate

Cookie Crust
- 2¼ **cups all-purpose flour**
- ½ **cup granulated sugar**
- 2 **teaspoons grated lemon peel**
  Pinch salt
- ¾ **cup cold butter *or* margarine, cut up**
- 2 **large egg yolks**
- 4 **tablespoons cold water**
- ½ **teaspoon vanilla extract**

Filling
- ¾ **cup granulated sugar**
- 3 **tablespoons quick-cooking tapioca**
- ¼ **teaspoon cinnamon**
- ¼ **teaspoon nutmeg**
- ⅛ **teaspoon salt**
- 4 **cups peeled and sliced ripe peaches**
- 2 **cups fresh huckleberries *or* blueberries**
- 1 **teaspoon fresh lemon juice**

1 For Cookie Crust, combine the flour, sugar, lemon peel, and salt in a medium bowl. Gradually add the butter, tossing gently until all pieces are coated with flour. With a pastry blender or 2 knives, cut in butter until mixture resembles coarse crumbs. Whisk together the egg yolks, water, and vanilla in a small bowl. Sprinkle onto flour mixture, 1 tablespoon at a time, tossing vigorously with a fork until pastry just begins to hold together. On a smooth surface, shape pastry into a ball, kneading lightly if necessary. Divide pastry into 2 balls, 1 slightly larger than the other. Flatten into 2 thick disks. Wrap tightly in plastic wrap and refrigerate 1 hour.

2 Preheat oven to 400°F. Roll the larger pastry disk between 2 sheets of floured wax paper into a 12-inch circle. Fit into a 9-inch pie plate. Trim edge. Bake for 10 minutes. Cool on a wire rack.

3 Meanwhile, for filling, combine the sugar, tapioca, cinnamon, nutmeg, and salt in a large saucepan. Add the peaches. Bring to a boil, stirring, over high heat. Remove from heat and stir in the berries and lemon juice. Cool slightly.

4 Roll remaining pastry between 2 sheets of floured wax paper to a 10-inch circle. With a fluted pastry cutter or sharp knife, cut circle into ½-inch-wide strips. Spoon filling into pastry shell. Arrange strips over filling 1 inch apart in a lattice pattern. Trim lattice ends. Bake for 10 minutes. Cover edge with foil to prevent over-browning. Bake for 30 to 35 minutes more or until filling is bubbly. Cool on a wire rack. Makes 8 servings.

PER SERVING		DAILY GOAL
Calories	485	2,000 (F), 2,500 (M)
Total fat	19 g	60 g or less (F), 70 g or less (M)
Saturated fat	11 g	20 g or less (F), 23 g or less (M)
Cholesterol	100 mg	300 mg or less
Sodium	232 mg	2,400 mg or less
Carbohydrates	76 g	250 g or more
Protein	5 g	55 g to 90 g

FRESH RASPBERRY PIE

The surprising addition of fruit pectin in this ruby red pie from the Gillespie Farms in North Yarmouth, Maine, helps the berries retain their just-picked taste.

Prep time: 35 minutes plus chilling
Baking time: 45 to 50 minutes
● *Degree of difficulty: moderate*

Double Flaky Pastry *or* Old-Fashioned Vinegar Pastry (recipes, page 8)
3   **tablespoons powdered fruit pectin (regular)**
1   **cup granulated sugar**
¼   **cup water**
3   **cups fresh raspberries**

1   Prepare Double Flaky Pastry or Old-Fashioned Vinegar Pastry as directed.

2   Preheat oven to 425°F. For filling, combine pectin, sugar, and water in a bowl. Stir in berries; let stand 10 minutes.

3   On a lightly floured surface, roll the larger disk into a 12-inch circle and fit into a 9-inch pie pan, leaving a 1-inch overhang. Spoon raspberry mixture into pastry shell. Brush overhang with water. Roll remaining pastry into a 10-inch circle. Cut vents and place on top of filling. Trim and flute the edge of pastry.

4   Bake 15 minutes. Reduce oven temperature to 350°F. Bake 30 to 35 minutes more or until filling is bubbly. Cool on a wire rack. Makes 8 servings.

PER SERVING		DAILY GOAL
Calories	400	2,000 (F), 2,500 (M)
Total fat	18 g	60 g or less (F), 70 g or less (M)
Saturated fat	9 g	20 g or less (F), 23 g or less (M)
Cholesterol	31 mg	300 mg or less
Sodium	262 mg	2,400 mg or less
Carbohydrates	57 g	250 g or more
Protein	4 g	55 g to 90 g

STRAWBERRY PIE

Prep time: 20 minutes
Baking time: 55 to 60 minutes
● *Degree of difficulty: moderate*

Double Flaky Pastry (recipe, page 8)
¾   **cup granulated sugar**
3   **tablespoons quick-cooking tapioca**
2   **tablespoons fresh lemon juice**
6   **cups halved fresh strawberries**
1   **tablespoon butter *or* margarine, cut up**
1   **large egg, lightly beaten**

1   Prepare Double Flaky Pastry as directed.

2   For filling, combine sugar, tapioca, and lemon juice in a bowl. Add berries, gently tossing to coat. Let stand 15 minutes.

3   Preheat oven to 450°F. On a lightly floured surface with a floured rolling pin, roll the larger disk into a 12-inch circle and fit into a 9-inch pie pan, leaving a 1-inch overhang. Spoon strawberry mixture into pastry shell. Dot with butter.

4   Roll remaining pastry into a 10-inch circle. Cut into ten 1-inch-wide strips and arrange in a lattice pattern on top of filling. Trim lattice ends and flute edge of pastry. Brush pastry with beaten egg.

5   Place pie on a cookie sheet and bake for 20 minutes. Reduce oven temperature to 375°F. Bake for 35 to 40 minutes more or until filling is bubbly and crust is golden. Cool on a wire rack at least 1 hour before serving. Makes 8 servings.

PER SERVING		DAILY GOAL
Calories	400	2,000 (F), 2,500 (M)
Total fat	19 g	60 g or less (F), 70 g or less (M)
Saturated fat	9 g	20 g or less (F), 23 g or less (M)
Cholesterol	61 mg	300 mg or less
Sodium	295 mg	2,400 mg or less
Carbohydrates	54 g	250 g or more
Protein	5 g	55 g to 90 g

BLACKBERRY CUSTARD PIE

Blackberry pie, plain or custard, is a favorite at the Eckert's Country Store and Farms in Belleville, Illinois. In this German custard pie, a regional specialty, a custard forms on the bottom during baking, while the luscious berries float to the top.

Prep time: 20 minutes plus chilling
Baking time: 68 to 73 minutes
○ *Degree of difficulty: easy*

Single Flaky Pastry (recipe, page 7)
2 **tablespoons all-purpose flour**
¾ **cup plus 2 tablespoons granulated sugar**
2 **large eggs, lightly beaten**
1 **cup milk**
3 **cups fresh blackberries**

1 Prepare Single Flaky Pastry as directed.

2 Preheat oven to 400°F. Line pastry shell with foil and fill with dried beans or uncooked rice. Bake for 10 minutes. Remove the foil and beans. Bake pastry for 3 minutes more. Cool completely on a wire rack.

3 For filling, combine the flour and sugar in a medium bowl. Whisk in the eggs and milk. Arrange the blackberries in the baked pastry shell. Carefully pour the egg filling over berries in pastry shell. Bake for 10 minutes. Reduce oven temperature to 350°F. Bake for 45 to 50 minutes more or until a small knife inserted in center of the filling comes out clean. Cool pie on a wire rack. Makes 8 servings.

PER SERVING		DAILY GOAL
Calories	280	2,000 (F), 2,500 (M)
Total fat	10 g	60 g or less (F), 70 g or less (M)
Saturated fat	5 g	20 g or less (F), 23 g or less (M)
Cholesterol	69 mg	300 mg or less
Sodium	143 mg	2,400 mg or less
Carbohydrates	44 g	250 g or more
Protein	5 g	55 g to 90 g

NOTES

FRESH APRICOT PHYLLO PIES

We love the tart-sweet flavor of fresh apricots, available in June and July, paired with this creamy mascarpone filling and crisp phyllo pastry.

Prep time: 20 minutes plus standing
Baking time: 6 to 8 minutes
⬤ *Degree of difficulty: moderate*

- 4 **sheets phyllo dough**
- 1 **tablespoon butter *or* margarine, melted**
- 3 **whole fresh apricots**
- 3 **tablespoons plus 1 teaspoon granulated sugar, divided**
- ½ **cup mascarpone cheese (*or* one 3-ounce package cream cheese mixed with 2 tablespoons sour cream)**
- 2 **teaspoons fresh lemon juice**
  Pinch salt
- 2 **tablespoons sliced almonds, toasted**

1 Preheat oven to 375°F. Brush each phyllo sheet with butter and stack. Cut phyllo lengthwise in half, then crosswise into thirds, making 6 squares. Line every other cup of a 12-cup muffin pan with phyllo. Bake for 6 to 8 minutes or until golden brown. Carefully remove phyllo cups from pan and cool on a wire rack.

2 Cut 2 of the apricots into ¼-inch slices and then toss with 3 tablespoons of the sugar. Let apricots stand for 30 minutes. Dice the remaining apricot and combine with the mascarpone, the remaining 1 teaspoon sugar, lemon juice, and salt in a mixing bowl.

3 To serve, fill each phyllo shell with the sliced apricots and 1 tablespoon of the mascarpone mixture. Sprinkle with almonds. Makes 6 servings.

PER SERVING		DAILY GOAL	
Calories	190	2,000 (F), 2,500 (M)	
Total fat	12 g	60 g or less (F), 70 g or less (M)	
Saturated fat	1 g	20 g or less (F), 23 g or less (M)	
Cholesterol	31 mg	300 mg or less	
Sodium	114 mg	2,400 mg or less	
Carbohydrates	17 g	250 g or more	
Protein	3 g	55 g to 90 g	

NOTES

PEACHES-AND-CREAM PHYLLO PIE

This pie crust is made from layers of baked phyllo and ground walnuts. Pile the flaky crust high with sliced fresh peaches just before serving. For a dessert that's truly distinctive, look for white peaches, usually sold at farmers' markets.

Prep time: 30 minutes
Baking time: 20 to 30 minutes
○ *Degree of difficulty: easy*

Pastry
- ¼ **cup walnuts, toasted**
- ¼ **cup plus 1 tablespoon granulated sugar, divided**
- ¼ **cup unsalted butter, melted (no substitutions)**
- 8 **sheets phyllo dough**

Filling
- ⅓ **cup mascarpone cheese *or* 1 package (3 ounces) cream cheese**
- 2 **tablespoons honey**
- 1 **tablespoon fresh lemon juice**
- 2 **tablespoons granulated sugar**
- 3 **pounds ripe peaches, peeled and sliced (6 cups)**

1 Preheat oven to 375°F. For pastry, process the walnuts with ¼ cup of the sugar in a food processor or blender until finely ground. Place a 9-inch pie plate on a cookie sheet and brush plate lightly with some of the melted butter. Place 1 phyllo sheet in plate and brush lightly with melted butter. Place another sheet on top in the opposite direction; brush with melted butter. Sprinkle a third of the nut mixture over phyllo. To form a rim, tuck in edges and crumple. Layer 2 more phyllo sheets, brushing with melted butter and sprinkling with nuts, then repeat. Top with remaining 2 phyllo sheets, brushing with melted butter and sprinkle with the remaining 1 tablespoon sugar. Crumple edges in.

2 Bake for 20 to 30 minutes or until golden. Cool on a wire rack. (Can be made ahead. Cover and let stand at room temperature up to 8 hours.)

3 Combine mascarpone and honey in a small bowl. (Can be made ahead. Cover and refrigerate up to 8 hours.)

4 Just before serving, combine lemon juice and sugar in a large bowl. Add the peaches and toss to combine. Spoon the mascarpone mixture into bottom of phyllo shell. Spoon peaches on top. Makes 6 servings.

PER SERVING		DAILY GOAL
Calories	390	2,000 (F), 2,500 (M)
Total fat	19 g	60 g or less (F), 70 g or less (M)
Saturated fat	5 g	20 g or less (F), 23 g or less (M)
Cholesterol	40 mg	300 mg or less
Sodium	133 mg	2,400 mg or less
Carbohydrates	55 g	250 g or more
Protein	5 g	55 g to 90 g

WHAT A PEACH!

The peak season for peaches is from the end of May to October.

How to buy: Select peaches that are fully ripe. Look for ones that are plump, large, and firm but not hard, with no trace of green or soft spots. They should have a cream- or golden-colored skin, a sweet fragrance, and a well-defined crease down the side. Redness is not a sign of ripeness.

How to ripen: Store peaches at room temperature for a day or two away from sunlight, or in a loosely closed paper bag or ripening bowl.

How to peel: Immerse a peach in boiling water for 20 to 30 seconds, then remove it with a slotted spoon and plunge it immediately into cold water. The skins should slip off.

43

SWEET AND

SILKY PIES

Slightly decadent and wonderfully creamy, this collection of pies is serious. Praline Banana and Coconut Cream pies, billowy Strawberry and Tropical Chiffon pies, and frozen Raspberry Ribbon and Chocolate Turtle pies are the perfect fix when you're feeling a little naughty. Go ahead, indulge with the sinful Red, White, and Blue Banana-Split Pie, tangy Lemon Meringue Pie, or Butterfinger Candy Pie and leave the guilt behind.

CLASSIC CHOCOLATE CREAM PIE

Chocolate doesn't get any better than this: a coal-black pudding nestled in a crisp crust and topped with sweet whipped cream. Even eating this filling plain is pure pleasure!

Prep time: 20 minutes plus chilling
Baking time: 20 to 22 minutes
○ *Degree of difficulty: easy*

Fully Baked Flaky Pastry
(recipe, page 7)
1 **cup granulated sugar**
¼ **cup cornstarch**
¼ **teaspoon salt**
2¾ **cups milk**
3 **large egg yolks**
3 **squares (3 ounces) unsweetened**
    chocolate, coarsely chopped
1 **tablespoon butter** *or* **margarine**
1 **teaspoon vanilla extract**
1 **cup heavy** *or* **whipping cream**
2 **tablespoons confectioners' sugar**

1 Prepare Fully Baked Flaky Pastry as directed.

2 For filling, combine the granulated sugar, cornstarch, and salt in a large saucepan. Gradually whisk in the milk until smooth. Bring to a boil over medium-high heat, stirring gently, then boil 1 minute. Remove from heat.

3 Beat the egg yolks lightly in a small bowl. Gradually whisk in 1 cup of the hot filling mixture. Return all of the filling to the saucepan, whisking constantly. Return to a boil and boil for 1 minute more. Remove from heat. Whisk in the chocolate, butter, and vanilla until completely smooth. Pour the filling into the baked pastry shell. Cool for 15 minutes on a wire rack. Cover the surface of the filling with wax paper or plastic wrap and refrigerate at least 3 hours.

4 Just before serving, in a large chilled mixing bowl, beat the heavy cream and confectioners' sugar until soft peaks form. Remove the wax paper from the filling and spread the whipped cream over the pie. Makes 8 servings.

PER SERVING		DAILY GOAL
Calories	555	2,000 (F), 2,500 (M)
Total Fat	35 g	60 g or less (F), 70 g or less (M)
Saturated fat	19 g	20 g or less (F), 23 g or less (M)
Cholesterol	159 mg	300 mg or less
Sodium	295 mg	2,400 mg or less
Carbohydrates	56 g	250 g or more
Protein	8 g	55 g to 90 g

ALL ABOUT CORNSTARCH

To make a smooth and creamy filling, combine cornstarch with sugar and other dry ingredients before adding the cold liquid. Gradually stir in the liquid until the mixture is completely smooth. It's important to always stir the filling constantly but gently over moderate heat. (Stirring too vigorously can cause the mixture to break down. Cooking it at too high a temperature can cause lumps and curdling if the filling contains eggs.) Once the cornstarch mixture has reached a full boil, continue to boil for one minute longer and remove from the heat.

COCONUT CREAM PIE

Here's a custard and cream classic packed with tender coconut in the filling and crisp toasted coconut on the top.

Prep time: 20 minutes plus chilling
Baking time: 20 to 22 minutes
○ *Degree of difficulty: easy*

Fully Baked Flaky Pastry
  (recipe, page 7)
⅔ **cup granulated sugar**
¼ **cup cornstarch**
¼ **teaspoon salt**
2½ **cups milk**
½ **cup heavy *or* whipping cream**
3 **large egg yolks**
1⅓ **cups shredded coconut**
1 **tablespoon butter *or* margarine**
2 **teaspoons vanilla extract**
¾ **cup heavy *or* whipping cream**
½ **cup shredded coconut, toasted**

1 Prepare Fully Baked Flaky Pastry as directed.

2 For filling, combine the sugar, cornstarch, and salt in a large saucepan.

Gradually whisk in the milk and cream until smooth. Bring to a boil over medium-high heat, stirring gently, then boil for 1 minute. Remove from heat.

3 Beat the egg yolks lightly in a small bowl. Gradually whisk in 1 cup of the hot filling mixture. Return all of the filling to the saucepan, whisking constantly. Return to a boil and boil for 1 minute more. Remove from heat. Stir in the coconut, butter, and vanilla until blended. Pour the filling into the baked pastry shell. Cool 15 minutes on a wire rack. Cover surface of filling with wax paper or plastic wrap and refrigerate at least 3 hours.

4 Just before serving, in a large chilled mixing bowl, beat the heavy cream until soft peaks form. Remove the wax paper from the filling and spread whipped cream over pie. Sprinkle top with the toasted coconut. Makes 8 servings.

PER SERVING		DAILY GOAL	
Calories	565	2,000 (F), 2,500 (M)	
Total fat	37 g	60 g or less (F), 70 g or less (M)	
Saturated fat	23 g	20 g or less (F), 23 g or less (M)	
Cholesterol	168 mg	300 mg or less	
Sodium	336 mg	2,400 mg or less	
Carbohydrates	51 g	250 g or more	
Protein	7 g	55 g to 90 g	

PRALINE-BANANA CREAM PIE

Prep time: 35 minutes plus chilling
Baking time: 23 to 25 minutes
Degree of difficulty: moderate

Pastry
- ⅓ cup pecan halves, lightly toasted
- 3 tablespoons granulated sugar
- 1 cup plus 2 tablespoons all-purpose flour
- ¼ teaspoon salt
  Pinch cinnamon
- 5 tablespoons cold butter, cut up (no substitutions)
- 1 tablespoon cold vegetable shortening
- 3 to 4 tablespoons cold water
- 1 large egg

Filling
- ½ cup packed brown sugar
- ⅓ cup cornstarch
  Pinch salt
- 2⅔ cups half-and-half *or* light cream
- 4 large egg yolks
- 2 teaspoons vanilla extract

- 2 tablespoons butter
- 2 ripe bananas, sliced

Whipped Cream
- 1 cup heavy *or* whipping cream
- 2 tablespoons granulated sugar
- 2 tablespoons amber rum
- ⅛ teaspoon cinnamon

1 For pastry, combine pecans and granulated sugar in a food processor and process until fine. Combine nut mixture with flour, salt, and cinnamon. Gradually add butter and shortening, tossing until coated with flour. Cut in butter and shortening. Add cold water, 1 tablespoon at a time, tossing vigorously with a fork until pastry just begins to hold together. Shape pastry into a ball and flatten into a thick disk. Wrap and chill 2 hours or overnight.

2 On a floured surface, roll pastry into a 14-inch circle; fit into a 10-inch pie pan. Trim and flute edge. Prick bottom with a fork. Refrigerate 30 minutes. For glaze, beat together the egg and 1 tablespoon water. Adjust oven rack to lowest position. Preheat oven to 400°F. Line pastry shell with foil and fill with dried beans or uncooked rice. Bake 15 minutes. Remove foil and beans. Brush with glaze; bake pas-

try 8 to 10 minutes or until golden brown. Cool on a wire rack.

3 For filling, combine brown sugar, cornstarch, and a pinch of salt in a saucepan. Whisk in half-and-half. Bring to a boil over medium heat, stirring, then boil 1 minute. Remove from heat.

4 Beat egg yolks. Gradually whisk in 1 cup of hot filling mixture. Return all filling to saucepan, whisking. Cook 2 minutes, whisking. *(Do not boil.)* Remove filling from heat and whisk in vanilla and butter until smooth. Cool 10 minutes. Arrange bananas in pastry shell; top with filling. Cover surface of filling with plastic wrap. Chill 3 hours or until filling is firm.

5 For Whipped Cream, beat the heavy cream in a mixing bowl until soft peaks form. Beat in sugar, rum, and cinnamon; continue to beat until stiff peaks form. Spoon into a pastry bag fitted with a star tip and pipe over pie. Serves 10.

PER SERVING		DAILY GOAL	
Calories	466	2,000 (F), 2,500 (M)	
Total fat	30 g	60 g or less (F), 70 g or less (M)	
Saturated fat	16 g	20 g or less (F), 23 g or less (M)	
Cholesterol	184 mg	300 mg or less	
Sodium	199 mg	2,400 mg or less	
Carbohydrates	41 g	250 g or more	
Protein	6 g	55 g to 90 g	

CHOCOLATE SEDUCTION PIE

Adapted from Bally's Park Place in Atlantic City, this pie is packed with chocolate. The trick to working with a large amount of chocolate is to maintain a velvety smoothness, so avoid overchilling and overbeating, which can cause the chocolate to become grainy.

Prep time: 30 minutes plus chilling
Baking time: 10 minutes
O *Degree of difficulty: easy*

Crust
1½ **cups graham cracker crumbs**
½ **cup finely chopped pecans**
      (optional)
1 **tablespoon granulated sugar**
¼ **cup butter, melted**

Filling
1¼ **cups heavy *or* whipping cream**
⅓ **cup milk**
½ **cup granulated sugar**
¼ **cup butter, cut up**
      (no substitutions)

16 **squares (16 ounces) semisweet chocolate, coarsely chopped**
      Sweetened whipped cream and chocolate shavings, for garnish

1 Preheat oven to 350°F. For crust, combine the graham cracker crumbs, pecans (if desired), sugar, and butter in a small bowl until crumbs are evenly moistened. Press into the bottom and up the sides of a 9-inch pie pan. Bake for 10 minutes. Cool pie completely on a wire rack.

2 For filling, bring the cream, milk, sugar, and butter to a boil in a large saucepan over medium-high heat. Remove from heat and stir in the chocolate until smooth. Place the saucepan in a large bowl filled with ice water. Chill, stirring occasionally, until cold, about 10 minutes. Remove from ice water. Transfer filling to a large mixing bowl and beat at medium speed about 1 minute or to soft peaks. *(Do not overbeat.)*

3 Pour filling into prepared crust. Refrigerate until firm, 4 hours or overnight. To serve, decorate pie with whipped cream and chocolate shavings. Makes 12 servings.

PER SERVING		DAILY GOAL
Calories	433	2,000 (F), 2,500 (M)
Total Fat	29 g	60 g or less (F), 70 g or less (M)
Saturated fat	17 g	20 g or less (F), 23 g or less (M)
Cholesterol	56 mg	300 mg or less
Sodium	185 mg	2,400 mg or less
Carbohydrates	45 g	250 g or more
Protein	3 g	55 g to 90 g

CHOCOLATE TURTLE PIE

This Southern-style specialty, made of caramel, pecans, and chocolate wrapped in a cookie crust, is a signature dessert at the landmark Grand & Wells Restaurant and Tap in Chicago.

Prep time: 30 minutes plus cooling
and chilling
Baking time: 10 minutes
O *Degree of difficulty: easy*

Cookie Crust
2 **cups chocolate sandwich cookie crumbs (18 cookies)**
¼ **cup butter *or* margarine, melted**

Caramel Filling
- 1 **cup caramel candies (20)**
- ¼ **cup heavy or whipping cream**
- 2 **cups pecan pieces**

Topping
- ¾ **cup (4 ounces) semisweet chocolate chips or 4 ounces semisweet chocolate, coarsely chopped**
- ¼ **cup heavy or whipping cream**

1 Preheat oven to 375°F. For Cookie Crust, combine the cookie crumbs and butter in a medium bowl. Press evenly in bottom and up the sides of a 9-inch tart pan or pie plate. Bake for 10 minutes. If necessary, press crust into place with a wooden spoon. Cool on a wire rack.

2 For Caramel Filling, melt the caramels, stirring frequently, in a heavy saucepan over low heat. Stir in the cream. Remove from heat and stir in the pecans. Spread evenly in prepared crust. Refrigerate 10 minutes or until set.

3 For topping, melt the chocolate in a double boiler over simmering water. Stir in the cream. Drizzle over filling. Refrigerate at least 1 hour. Makes 12 servings.

PER SERVING		DAILY GOAL
Calories	360	2,000 (F), 2,500 (M)
Total fat	27 g	60 g or less (F), 70 g or less (M)
Saturated fat	9 g	20 g or less (F), 23 g or less (M)
Cholesterol	25 mg	300 mg or less
Sodium	166 mg	2,400 mg or less
Carbohydrates 3	1 g	250 g or more
Protein	3 g	55 g to 90 g

BUTTERFINGER CANDY PIE

When he was growing up, Dean Fearing thought that candy bars were the ultimate dessert—all those flavors in one package! As the chef at the elegant Mansion at Turtle Creek in Dallas, he takes his childhood sweet tooth to a higher level.

Prep time: 30 minutes plus cooling
Baking time: 45 minutes
○ *Degree of difficulty: easy*

Fully Baked Flaky Pastry (recipe, page 7)
- 2 **large eggs**
- ¼ **cup water**
- 1 **cup granulated sugar**
- ¼ **cup all-purpose flour**
- ¼ **teaspoon salt**
- ½ **cup unsalted butter (no substitutions)**
- 8 **Butterfinger candy bars (2.1 ounces each), coarsely chopped, divided**
- **Whipped cream, for garnish**

1 Prepare Fully Baked Flaky Pastry as directed.

2 For filling, beat eggs lightly in a large bowl. Stir in water, sugar, flour, and salt until well combined. Melt the butter in a small saucepan over low heat. Stir melted butter into batter. Stir in 6 of the chopped candy bars. (Can be made ahead. Cover and chill up to 24 hours.)

3 Preheat oven to 325°F. Pour filling into baked pastry shell and bake for 45 minutes or until barely set. Cool pie on a wire rack. Cover and refrigerate overnight. Garnish with the whipped cream and remaining 2 chopped candy bars. Makes 10 servings.

PER SERVING		DAILY GOAL
Calories	337	2,000 (F), 2,500 (M)
Total fat	20 g	60 g or less (F), 70 g or less (M)
Saturated fat	11 g	20 g or less (F), 23 g or less (M)
Cholesterol	86 mg	300 mg or less
Sodium	193 mg	2,400 mg or less
Carbohydrates	37 g	250 g or more
Protein	4 g	55 g to 90 g

LEMON MERINGUE PIE

Lemon Meringue is ultimately the queen of pies. To prevent the meringue from shrinking away from the filling, keep the filling warm in the saucepan. *Also pictured on page 44.*

Prep time: 35 minutes plus chilling
Baking time: 8 minutes
Degree of difficulty: moderate

Fully Baked Flaky Pastry (recipe, page 7)

Filling
1¼	**cups granulated sugar**
⅓	**cup cornstarch**
1½	**cups water**
4	**large egg yolks**
½	**cup fresh lemon juice**
2	**teaspoons grated lemon peel**
1	**tablespoon butter *or* margarine**

Meringue
4	**large egg whites, at room temperature**
⅓	**cup granulated sugar**

1 Prepare Fully Baked Flaky Pastry as directed.

2 Preheat oven to 350°F. For filling, combine the sugar and cornstarch in a large saucepan. Gradually whisk in the water until smooth. Bring to a boil over medium-high heat, stirring, then boil 1 minute. Remove from heat.

3 Beat the egg yolks in a small bowl. Gradually whisk in 1 cup of the hot filling mixture. Return all of the filling to the saucepan, whisking constantly. Whisk in the lemon juice and peel and boil for 1 minute more. Remove from heat and stir in the butter until smooth. Cover surface of filling with plastic wrap.

4 For meringue, beat the egg whites in a large mixing bowl at medium-high speed to soft peaks. Gradually beat in the sugar 1 tablespoon at a time, then continue to beat until stiff peaks form.

5 Pour the hot filling into the baked pastry shell. Spread meringue over filling, sealing to the edge. Bake for 6 to 8 minutes until top is golden. Cool for 30 minutes on a wire rack. Refrigerate until filling is firm, at least 4 hours. Makes 8 servings.

PER SERVING		DAILY GOAL
Calories	417	2,000 (F), 2,500 (M)
Total fat	16 g	60 g or less (F), 70 g or less (M)
Saturated fat	8 g	20 g or less (F), 23 g or less (M)
Cholesterol	133 mg	300 mg or less
Sodium	202 mg	2,400 mg or less
Carbohydrates	64 g	250 g or more
Protein	6 g	55 g to 90 g

MILE-HIGH MERINGUE TOPPING

To prevent the meringue from shrinking or weeping, always apply it to the pie filling while the filling is still hot. Simply prepare the filling first, then cover it and keep it warm while beating the egg whites and sugar for the meringue. Make sure that the meringue is completely spread all over the surface of the pie filling and that it touches the edge of the pie crust to form a tight seal. Bake the pie immediately, just until decorative peaks turn a golden brown, rotating your pie if necessary to evenly brown the meringue. Cool pie for 30 minutes on a wire rack, then refrigerate.

BUTTERMILK PIE

This custard pie is a specialty of Linda Hodges, selected as the best cook in town by Florida's Orlando Sentinel. A Southern favorite, we think you'll love this pie's farm-fresh flavor, too.

Prep time: 15 minutes
Baking time: 60 to 67 minutes
○ *Degree of difficulty: easy*

Single Flaky Pastry (recipe, page 7)
1 **cup granulated sugar**
2 **tablespoons all-purpose flour**
¼ **teaspoon nutmeg**
3 **large eggs**
1 **cup buttermilk**
⅓ **cup butter, melted, cooled to room temperature (no substitutions)**
1 **teaspoon vanilla extract**
½ **cup flaked coconut**
½ **cup chopped pecans**

1 Prepare Single Flaky Pastry as directed. Freeze for 15 minutes.

2 Preheat oven to 425°F. Line the frozen pastry shell with foil and fill with dried beans or uncooked rice. Bake for 12 minutes. Remove foil and beans. Bake pastry for 8 to 10 minutes more or until deep golden. Cool completely on a wire rack.

3 Reduce oven temperature to 350°F. Combine the sugar, flour, and nutmeg in a large mixing bowl. With a mixer at medium speed, beat in the eggs until smooth. Beat in the buttermilk, butter, and vanilla to blend. Pour mixture into the baked pastry shell, then sprinkle the top with the coconut and pecans.

4 Bake for 40 to 45 minutes or until filling is just set. Cool pie on a wire rack. Serve at room temperature or chilled. Makes 8 servings.

PER SERVING		DAILY GOAL
Calories	470	2,000 (F), 2,500 (M)
Total Fat	28 g	60 g or less (F), 70 g or less (M)
Saturated fat	13 g	20 g or less (F), 23 g or less (M)
Cholesterol	125 mg	300 mg or less
Sodium	301 mg	2,400 mg or less
Carbohydrates	50 g	250 g or more
Protein	7 g	55 g to 90 g

PERFECT WHIPPED CREAM

For the best results when whipping cream, first chill the mixing bowl and beaters in the freezer for 5 minutes. Begin to beat the cream at medium speed until soft peaks form, then add sugar or vanilla extract for sweetened whipped cream, if desired. Increase the speed to medium-high and continue to beat the cream until stiff peaks form when the beaters are raised. Be careful not to overbeat the cream or it may become grainy.

GRASSHOPPER PIE

The chocolate crumb crust is a must, and for best flavor, use good-quality liqueurs.

Prep time: 55 minutes plus chilling
Baking time: 10 minutes
● *Degree of difficulty: moderate*

Chocolate Crumb Crust

1½ cups (30 cookies) chocolate wafer crumbs
¼ cup butter or margarine, melted

Filling

1 envelope unflavored gelatin
¾ cup milk
4 large eggs, separated, at room temperature
¾ cup granulated sugar, divided
⅛ teaspoon salt
3 tablespoons crème de menthe liqueur
3 tablespoons white crème de menthe liqueur
½ cup heavy *or* whipping cream, beaten until stiff
   Whipped cream and chocolate shavings, for garnish (optional)

1 Preheat oven to 350°F. For Chocolate Crumb Crust, combine the cookie crumbs and butter in a small bowl until crumbs are evenly moistened. Press into the bottom and up the sides of a 9-inch pie pan. Bake for 10 minutes. Cool completely on a wire rack.

2 For filling, sprinkle the gelatin over the milk in a double boiler, then set aside and let soften 3 minutes. Whisk in the egg yolks, ½ cup of the sugar, and the salt. Cook over simmering water, stirring constantly, about 8 minutes or until gelatin is completely dissolved. Remove from heat and stir in the liqueurs. Transfer mixture to a large bowl and place in a larger bowl filled with ice water. Cool, stirring occasionally, about 10 minutes or until the mixture mounds slightly when dropped from a spoon.

3 Meanwhile, beat the egg whites in a large mixing bowl to soft peaks. Gradually beat in the remaining ¼ cup sugar until stiff peaks form. Remove custard mixture from ice water and fold in beaten whites with a rubber spatula. Fold in the whipped cream until blended. Return to ice bath for 5 to 10 minutes or until mixture mounds when dropped from a spoon. Spoon the filling into the prepared crust. Smooth the top with a spatula. Refrigerate until filling is firm, at least 4 hours. Garnish with whipped cream and chocolate shavings, if desired. Makes 8 servings.

PER SERVING		DAILY GOAL	
Calories	375	2,000 (F), 2,500 (M)	
Total fat	18 g	60 g or less (F), 70 g or less (M)	
Saturated fat	9 g	20 g or less (F), 23 g or less (M)	
Cholesterol	145 mg	300 mg or less	
Sodium	275 mg	2,400 mg or less	
Carbohydrates	42 g	250 g or more	
Protein	6 g	55 g to 90 g	

ALL ABOUT GELATIN

When preparing a chiffon pie, dissolving the gelatin correctly is a crucial first step. Always start by sprinkling the gelatin over cold liquid, then allow the mixture to stand for 5 minutes so the granules will soften. When heating, stir constantly with a spatula, 2 to 3 minutes. To make sure the gelatin is completely dissolved, run your finger along the surface of the spatula. It should feel completely smooth. If there are still granules, continue to heat another minute.

STRAWBERRIES 'N' CREAM ANGEL PIE

You won't believe how easy this do-ahead pie from the *Winterthur's Culinary Collection* community cookbook is. We love this dessert with fresh blueberries and raspberries, too.

Total prep time: 15 minutes plus cooling

O *Degree of difficulty: easy*

- 5 large egg whites, at room temperature
- ½ teaspoon cream of tartar
- ¼ teaspoon salt
- 1½ cups granulated sugar
- 1 teaspoon vanilla extract
- 2 pints fresh strawberries, cleaned and stems removed
- 1 cup heavy *or* whipping cream, beaten until stiff

1 Preheat oven to 450°F. Grease a 9-inch pie plate or 9-inch springform pan.

2 Combine the egg whites, cream of tartar, and salt in a large mixing bowl. Beat at high speed until foamy. Gradually beat in the sugar, 1 tablespoon at a time. Beat in the vanilla then continue to beat for 5 minutes more. Spread mixture evenly in prepared pie plate.

3 Turn off heat. Put the pie in the oven, leaving it overnight. *(Do not open oven door.)* To serve, fill with strawberries and top with whipped cream. Makes 8 servings.

PER SERVING		DAILY GOAL
Calories	285	2,000 (F), 2,500 (M)
Total fat	11 g	60 g or less (F), 70 g or less (M)
Saturated fat	7 g	20 g or less (F), 23 g or less (M)
Cholesterol	41 mg	300 mg or less
Sodium	114 mg	2,400 mg or less
Carbohydrates	44 g	250 g or more
Protein	3 g	55 g to 90 g

ANGEL PECAN PIE

This whipped cream pie is from Ann Preaus, selected as the best cook in town by the Times-Picayune in New Orleans. You'll never guess the secret ingredient in this crunchy crust—Ritz crackers!

Prep time: 30 minutes plus cooling
Baking time: 45 minutes

O *Degree of difficulty: easy*

- 1½ cups pecans
- 5 large egg whites, at room temperature
- 1½ cups granulated sugar
- 1½ teaspoons vanilla extract
- 1½ cups crumbled Ritz crackers
- 1 cup heavy *or* whipping cream
- 2 tablespoons confectioners' sugar
  Chocolate shavings, for garnish

1 Preheat oven to 350°F. Spread the pecans on a baking pan and bake for 8 to 10 minutes or until fragrant and toasted. Cool completely and chop coarsely.

2 Line the bottom and sides of a 9-inch springform pan with a large sheet of parchment paper or foil, creasing paper to line the side of the pan.

3 Beat the egg whites in a large mixing bowl at medium speed to soft peaks. Beat in granulated sugar, 1 tablespoon at a time. Increase speed to high and continue to beat until very stiff and glossy, about 1 minute more. Beat in the vanilla. Gently fold in the pecans and cracker crumbs with a rubber spatula. Spoon into prepared pan and bake for 30 minutes. Cover top of pan loosely with foil and bake for 15 minutes more. Cool in pan on a wire rack. (Can be made ahead. Cover and store at room temperature up to 2 days.)

4 To serve, remove sides of pan and invert pie onto a plate. Peel off paper and invert again onto a serving plate. Beat the cream with confectioners' sugar in a large mixing bowl to stiff peaks and spread over pie. Garnish with chocolate shavings. Makes 12 servings.

PER SERVING		DAILY GOAL
Calories	315	2,000 (F), 2,500 (M)
Total fat	19 g	60 g or less (F), 70 g or less (M)
Saturated fat	5 g	20 g or less (F), 23 g or less (M)
Cholesterol	27 mg	300 mg or less
Sodium	120 mg	2,400 mg or less
Carbohydrates	35 g	250 g or more
Protein	4 g	55 g to 90 g

TROPICAL CHIFFON PIE

A dazzling dessert flavored with cream of coconut, rum, bananas, and pineapple will make quite a splash at any festive occasion.

Prep time: 1 hour plus chilling
Baking time: 23 to 25 minutes
● *Degree of difficulty: moderate*

Fully Baked Flaky Pastry (recipe, page 7)
1   **envelope plus 1 teaspoon unflavored gelatin**

3   **tablespoons dark rum**
2   **tablespoons cold water**
1   **small can (8¾ ounces) cream of coconut**
½   **cup milk**
3   **large eggs, separated, at room temperature**
1   **tablespoon granulated sugar**
1   **cup heavy *or* whipping cream**
1   **can (8 ounces) pineapple slices in unsweetened juice, drained and diced**
½   **cup shredded coconut**
1   **large banana, sliced**
1   **cup sliced fresh strawberries**
¼   **cup shredded coconut, toasted**
¼   **cup macadamia nuts *or* chopped, toasted pecans**

1 Prepare Fully Baked Flaky Pastry as directed.

2 For filling, sprinkle the gelatin over the rum and water in a small bowl to soften. Meanwhile, heat the cream of coconut and milk in a medium saucepan to boiling. Whisk the egg yolks lightly in a medium bowl. Gradually whisk in hot coconut mixture. Return to saucepan and cook, stirring constantly, over medium heat about 3 minutes or until mixture thickens slightly and

coats the back of a spoon. *(Do not boil.)* Remove from heat and add gelatin mixture, stirring about 1 minute or until gelatin is completely dissolved.

3 Transfer custard to a large bowl. Place bowl in a larger bowl filled with ice water. Stir frequently for 5 to 10 minutes or until cold and just beginning to set. Immediately remove from ice bath.

4 Meanwhile, beat the egg whites in a large mixing bowl until foamy. Add the sugar and continue beating until stiff. Whisk a third of the whites into custard, then fold in remaining whites with a rubber spatula. Beat the cream in the same mixing bowl until stiff. Fold whipped cream into custard. Fold in the pineapple, coconut, and banana. Spoon into baked pastry shell. Top with the strawberries, coconut, and nuts. Cover with plastic wrap and refrigerate at least 3 hours. Makes 10 servings.

PER SERVING		DAILY GOAL
Calories	425	2,000 (F), 2,500 (M)
Total fat	30 g	60 g or less (F), 70 g or less (M)
Saturated fat	18 g	20 g or less (F), 23 g or less (M)
Cholesterol	117 mg	300 mg or less
Sodium	191 mg	2,400 mg or less
Carbohydrates	30 g	250 g or more
Protein	7 g	55 g to 90 g

STRAWBERRY CHIFFON PIE

The essence of springtime is this strawberry and whipped cream filling that's light as a cloud.

Prep time: 50 minutes plus chilling
Baking time: 18 minutes
● *Degree of difficulty: moderate*

Vanilla Crumb Crust
- ⅓ **cup blanched slivered almonds**
- 2½ **cups vanilla wafer cookies**
- ¼ **cup butter *or* margarine, melted**

Strawberry Filling
- 2 **packages (10 ounces each) frozen strawberries in light syrup, thawed**
- 1 **tablespoon fresh lemon juice**
- 1 **envelope plus 1 teaspoon gelatin**
- 3 **large egg whites, at room temperature**
- ⅓ **cup granulated sugar**
- ½ **cup heavy *or* whipping cream, beaten until stiff**
  Whipped cream, fresh strawberries, and mint leaves, for garnish

1 Preheat oven to 350° F. For Vanilla Crumb Crust, place the almonds on a small cookie sheet and toast, stirring once, for 8 minutes or until golden. Cool. (Leave oven on.) Combine nuts and vanilla wafers in a food processor and process to fine crumbs. Add butter and pulse about 10 minutes or until crumbs are evenly moistened. Press along bottom and sides of a 9-inch pie plate. Bake for 10 minutes or until golden. Cool on a wire rack.

2 For Strawberry Filling, strain the syrup from the strawberries through a sieve into a small saucepan and set aside. Transfer berries to a large bowl and crush with a potato masher or fork, then stir in the lemon juice and set aside.

3 Sprinkle the gelatin over reserved syrup in the saucepan and let soften 3 minutes. Cook, stirring, over low heat about 10 minutes or until gelatin is completely dissolved. Stir syrup mixture into crushed strawberries. Place bowl in larger bowl filled with ice water. Cool, stirring occasionally, for 3 to 5 minutes or until mixture mounds slightly when dropped from a spoon.

4 Meanwhile, beat the egg whites to soft peaks in a large mixing bowl. Gradually beat in the sugar until stiff peaks form. Remove strawberry mixture from ice water, then fold in beaten whites. Fold in the whipped cream until blended. Spoon filling into cooled crust and smooth top with a spatula. Refrigerate at least 3 hours or until filling is firm. Garnish with whipped cream, strawberries, and mint leaves. Makes 8 servings.

PER SERVING		DAILY GOAL
Calories	311	2,000 (F), 2,500 (M)
Total fat	17 g	60 g or less (F), 70 g or less (M)
Saturated fat	8 g	20 g or less (F), 23 g or less (M)
Cholesterol	36 mg	300 mg or less
Sodium	137 mg	2,400 mg or less
Carbohydrates	39 g	250 g or more
Protein	5 g	55 g to 90 g

NOTES

_____

_____

_____

_____

_____

_____

_____

CHOCOLATE-PEANUT BUTTER ICE CREAM PIE

At K.C. Masterpiece Barbeque & Grill in Kansas City, there's no such thing as a meal that's too hearty or a dessert that's too rich. Co-owner Rich Davis calls this a classic American dessert.

Prep time: 30 minutes plus freezing
Baking time: 10 minutes
O *Degree of difficulty: easy*

Crust
15 chocolate sandwich cookies
½ cup dry-roasted peanuts
¼ cup butter *or* margarine, melted

Filling
3 pints premium chocolate ice cream, softened
7 packages (1.8 ounces each) *or* 20 packages (6 ounces each) Reese's peanut butter cups, coarsely chopped
1 cup heavy *or* whipping cream
2 tablespoons confectioners' sugar

Sauce
1 jar (8 ounces) chocolate fudge topping
¼ cup strong, brewed coffee
2 tablespoons coffee-flavor liqueur

1 Preheat oven to 375°F. For crust, combine the cookies with the peanuts in a food processor and process to fine crumbs. Reserve 1 tablespoon of the crumbs for garnish. Combine the remaining crumbs with the melted butter in a medium bowl. Press along the bottom and up the sides of a 9-inch pie plate. Bake about 10 minutes or until set. If necessary, press into place with a wooden spoon. Cool on a wire rack.

2 For filling, combine the ice cream with the chopped peanut butter cups in a large bowl. Spoon into cooled crust. Cover and freeze for 6 hours or overnight.

3 Beat the cream with the sugar in a small mixing bowl to stiff peaks. Spoon or pipe whipped cream over pie, then sprinkle reserved crumbs on top.

4 For sauce, heat the fudge topping in a small saucepan until hot, then stir in the coffee and liqueur. Spoon sauce over pie. Makes 12 servings.

PER SERVING		DAILY GOAL
Calories	720	2,000 (F), 2,500 (M)
Total fat	41 g	60 g or less (F), 70 g or less (M)
Saturated fat	24 g	20 g or less (F), 23 g or less (M)
Cholesterol	87 mg	300 mg or less
Sodium	338 mg	2,400 mg or less
Carbohydrates	84 g	250 g or more
Protein	11 g	55 g to 90 g

NOTES

RED, WHITE, AND BLUE BANANA-SPLIT PIE

This summertime treat is wickedly delicious and thanks to the microwave, it's no sweat to make! Chocolate chips make the brownie layer extra chocolatey and super-rich.

Ⓜ *Microwave*
Prep time: 20 minutes
Cooking time: 14 to 16 minutes
Ⓞ *Degree of difficulty: easy*

Brownie Layer
- ½ cup butter *or* margarine
- 2 tablespoons vegetable oil
- ½ cup unsweetened cocoa powder
- 3 large eggs
- 1 cup granulated sugar
- ¾ cup all-purpose flour
- 1 teaspoon vanilla extract
- ¾ teaspoon baking powder
- ¼ teaspoon salt
- 1 cup semisweet chocolate chips (optional)

Blueberry Sauce
- 2 teaspoons cornstarch
- ¼ cup water
- ¼ cup granulated sugar
- 1 pint fresh blueberries
- 1 tablespoon fresh lemon juice
- 4 ripe bananas, sliced
- 4 scoops each vanilla, chocolate, and strawberry ice cream
- 1 cup marshmallow cream
- 8 fresh strawberries

1 For Brownie Layer, grease a 9-inch microwave-proof pie plate. Microwave the butter in a medium microwave-proof bowl on high (100% power) for 1 to 1½ minutes or until melted. Whisk in the oil and cocoa until smooth. Whisk in the eggs, then the sugar, flour, vanilla, baking powder, and salt. Stir in the chocolate chips, if desired. Spread into prepared pan. Microwave on medium (50% power) for 5 minutes, rotating pan halfway through. Rotate again and microwave on high (100% power) for 2 to 2½ minutes more or until the center of brownie is firm to the touch. Cool on a wire rack.

2 For Blueberry Sauce, dissolve the cornstarch in water in a medium microwave-proof bowl. Stir in the sugar and blueberries. Microwave on high (100% power) for 5 minutes or until boiling, stirring once. Microwave on high (100% power) 1 minute more. Stir in the lemon juice. Serve warm or at room temperature.

3 Arrange the bananas and ice cream on brownie layer. Spoon the marshmallow cream on top, drizzle with half of the Blueberry Sauce, and garnish with strawberries. Serve the remaining Blueberry Sauce on the side. Makes 8 servings.

PER SERVING		DAILY GOAL
Calories	650	2,000 (F), 2,500 (M)
Total fat	28 g	60 g or less (F), 70 g or less (M)
Saturated fat	13 g	20 g or less (F), 23 g or less (M)
Cholesterol	146 mg	300 mg or less
Sodium	335 mg	2,400 mg or less
Carbohydrates	98 g	250 g or more
Protein	9 g	55 g to 90 g

NOTES

RASPBERRY RIBBON MERINGUE PIE

A beauty from the deep freeze! We've layered ruby red raspberry purée with vanilla ice cream under a gorgeous meringue bonnet.

Ⓜ *Microwave*
Prep time: 40 minutes plus freezing
Baking time: 10 minutes
Ⓞ *Degree of difficulty: easy*

Chocolate Crumb Crust (see recipe for Grasshopper Pie, page 55)

Filling
- **2 cups fresh raspberries**
- **½ cup granulated sugar**
- **1 tablespoon cornstarch**
- **¼ cup butter *or* margarine, cut up**
- **2 pints premium vanilla ice cream**

Topping
- **4 large egg whites, at room temperature**
- **Pinch salt**
- **⅓ cup granulated sugar**
- **½ teaspoon vanilla extract**

1 Prepare Chocolate Crumb Crust as directed. Freeze crust for 1 hour.

2 For filling, place raspberries in a food processor or blender and purée. Strain raspberries through a fine sieve into a 4-cup microwave-proof measure. Stir in the sugar and cornstarch and add the butter. Cover with plastic wrap, turning back a section to vent. Microwave on high (100% power), stirring once, about 4 minutes or until thickened. Whisk until smooth, then cool to room temperature.

3 Soften 1 pint ice cream slightly. Quickly spread evenly over crust and cover with 1 cup raspberry purée. Freeze 30 minutes. Repeat layering process with remaining 1 pint ice cream and raspberry purée. Freeze for 30 minutes. Cover pie and freeze overnight.

4 Preheat oven to 450°F. For topping, beat the egg whites and salt in a large mixing bowl at medium speed until soft peaks form. Gradually beat in the sugar and vanilla and continue to beat at medium speed to stiff peaks.

5 Unwrap frozen pie. With a spatula, spread the meringue completely over top of pie, mounding more meringue in center.

Swirl through meringue with the back of a spoon to form decorative peaks. Bake about 2 minutes or until topping is browned. Immediately place in freezer and freeze at least 1 hour. (Can be made ahead. Cover and freeze up to 2 days.) Makes 12 servings.

PER SERVING		DAILY GOAL	
Calories	290	2,000 (F), 2,500 (M)	
Total Fat	14 g	60 g or less (F), 70 g or less (M)	
Saturated fat	8 g	20 g or less (F), 23 g or less (M)	
Cholesterol	40 mg	300 mg or less	
Sodium	224 mg	2,400 mg or less	
Carbohydrates	37 g	250 g or more	
Protein	4 g	55 g to 90 g	

NOTES

_____

_____

_____

_____

_____

_____

_____

GLORIOUS HOLIDAY

PIES AND TARTS

Here are pies to be thankful for…all the treasured nut, pumpkin, and winter fruit pies that hold center stage on the holiday dessert table. So come celebrate and cherish all our favorites—Maple-Butternut Tart with Glazed Pecans, Cranberry-Nut Pie, and Frozen Pumpkin Mousse Pie. Each pie is guaranteed to make your holiday memorable.

PUMPKIN CHEESECAKE PIE

Here's a do-ahead pie that's perfect for the holiday crowd. Simply prepare the filling the night before, cover and refrigerate, then return it to room temperature before filling the crumb crust and baking.

Prep time: 50 minutes
Baking time: 63 to 70 minutes
○ *Degree of difficulty: easy*

Crust

1	**cup graham cracker crumbs**
½	**cup ground pecans**
2	**tablespoons granulated sugar**
⅛	**teaspoon ginger**
¼	**cup butter *or* margarine**

Filling

¾	**cup firmly packed brown sugar**
1	**package (8 ounces) cream cheese, at room temperature**
1	**can (16 ounces) solid-pack pumpkin**
½	**cup heavy *or* whipping cream**
1	**teaspoon cinnamon**
½	**teaspoon ginger**
½	**teaspoon salt**
¼	**teaspoon nutmeg**
¼	**teaspoon cloves**
	Pinch freshly ground pepper
3	**large eggs**
	Pecan halves and sweetened whipped cream, for garnish (optional)

1 Preheat oven to 350°F. For crust, combine the cracker crumbs, pecans, sugar, and ginger in a medium bowl. Stir in the butter until crumbs are evenly moistened. Press evenly onto bottom and sides of a 9-inch pie plate. Bake for 8 to 10 minutes. Cool completely on a wire rack.

2 For filling, beat the brown sugar and cream cheese in a large mixing bowl until light and fluffy. Beat in the pumpkin, cream, cinnamon, ginger, salt, nutmeg, cloves, and pepper until smooth. With mixer at low speed, beat in the eggs, 1 at a time, until blended.

3 Pour filling into baked crust. Bake for 55 to 60 minutes or until a wooden toothpick inserted in center of filling comes out clean. Cool completely on a wire rack. Pipe edge with whipped cream and garnish with pecans, if desired. Makes 8 to 10 servings.

PER SERVING WITHOUT GARNISH		DAILY GOAL
Calories	390	2,000 (F), 2,500 (M)
Total fat	25 g	60 g or less (F), 70 g or less (M)
Saturated fat	13 g	20 g or less (F), 23 g or less (M)
Cholesterol	130 mg	300 mg or less
Sodium	364 mg	2,400 mg or less
Carbohydrates	37 g	250 g or more
Protein	6 g	55 g to 90 g

THE GREAT PUMPKIN

Canned pumpkin is one of the best ingredients we know for a fast and easy holiday pie filling. Be sure to purchase cans that say "solid-pack pumpkin" rather than "pumpkin pie filling" which contains additional spices.

NOTES

_____

_____

_____

_____

_____

FLUFFY PUMPKIN PIES

Here's a contribution from Julia Child—two pumpkin pies—enough to feed a crowd.

Prep time: 20 minutes plus chilling
Baking time: 45 to 50 minutes
○ *Degree of difficulty: easy*

Double Flaky Pastry *or* Old-Fashioned Vinegar Pastry (recipes, page 8)

2   **cans (16 ounces each) solid-pack pumpkin**
1   **cup heavy *or* whipping cream**
¾   **cup milk**
¾   **cup granulated sugar**
¾   **cup firmly packed brown sugar**
3   **tablespoons dark rum *or* bourbon**
2   **teaspoons ginger**
2   **teaspoons cinnamon**
1   **teaspoon salt**
¼   **teaspoon nutmeg**
¼   **teaspoon cloves**
4   **large egg yolks**
5   **large egg whites**

1   Prepare Double Flaky Pastry or Old-Fashioned Vinegar Pastry as directed, except divide dough in half and form into 2 thick disks the same size.

2   On a lightly floured surface with a floured rolling pin, roll each disk into an 11-inch circle. Fit circles into two 9-inch pie pans. Flute edges to form a high rim. Refrigerate 30 minutes.

3   Preheat oven to 450°F. Whisk together the pumpkin, cream, milk, granulated sugar, brown sugar, rum, ginger, cinnamon, salt, nutmeg, cloves, and egg yolks in a large bowl until smooth. Beat the egg whites in a mixing bowl until stiff but not dry. Gently fold the whites into the pumpkin mixture with a rubber spatula. Ladle into prepared pastry shells.

4   Bake pies for 15 minutes. Reduce oven temperature to 350°F. Bake for 15 minutes more or until a wooden toothpick inserted 2 inches from edge of pies comes out clean. Turn off oven. Leave the pies in the oven with the door ajar for 20 minutes. Serve warm or chilled. Makes 2 pies, 8 servings each.

PER SERVING		DAILY GOAL
Calories	310	2,000 (F), 2,500 (M)
Total fat	16 g	60 g or less (F), 70 g or less (M)
Saturated fat	8 g	20 g or less (F), 23 g or less (M)
Cholesterol	91 mg	300 mg or less
Sodium	302 mg	2,400 mg or less
Carbohydrates	37 g	250 g or more
Protein	5 g	55 g to 90 g

NOTES

_____

_____

_____

_____

_____

_____

_____

_____

_____

_____

EXTRAORDINARY SWEET POTATO PIE

This recipe was given to us by dancer Judith Jamison, former star of the Alvin Ailey American Dance Theater.

Prep time: 45 minutes plus chilling
Baking time: 55 to 67 minutes
Degree of difficulty: moderate

Double Flaky Pastry
   (recipe, page 8)
¼ **cup raisins**
¼ **cup cognac *or* brandy**
2 **large sweet potatoes (about 1 pound), peeled and cut into large chunks**
4 **tablespoons butter, softened**
½ **cup granulated sugar**
3 **large eggs, separated**
½ **cup evaporated milk**
1 **can (8 ounces) crushed pineapple in unsweetened juice, drained**
¾ **teaspoon cinnamon**
⅛ **teaspoon nutmeg**
20 **miniature marshmallows**
8 **large marshmallows, halved**

1 Prepare Double Flaky Pastry as directed, except form dough into only 1 disk.

2 Combine the raisins and cognac in a small bowl and let stand 1 hour to plump.

3 On a lightly floured surface with a floured rolling pin, roll pastry into a 12-inch circle and fit into a 10-inch pie pan, leaving a 2-inch overhang. Flute edge of pastry, then prick bottom with a fork. Refrigerate 30 minutes.

4 Preheat oven to 400°F. Bake the pastry shell for 10 to 12 minutes or until lightly golden. Remove pastry from the oven and cool on a wire rack. Reduce the oven temperature to 350°F.

5 Meanwhile, cook the sweet potatoes in lightly salted water about 20 minutes or until soft. Drain well in a colander. Mash the sweet potatoes with the butter in a large bowl until smooth. Stir in the sugar and egg yolks. Stir in the raisins with their liquid, the evaporated milk, pineapple, cinnamon, and nutmeg. In a clean bowl, beat the egg whites until stiff but not dry. Fold egg whites into sweet potatoes with a rubber spatula. Pour filling into crust.

6 Bake for 40 to 50 minutes or until a small knife inserted in center comes out clean. Arrange the small and large marshmallows on top of pie. Bake for 5 minutes more or until marshmallows are lightly browned. Serve warm or at room temperature. Makes 10 to 12 servings.

PER SERVING		DAILY GOAL	
Calories	380	2,000 (F), 2,500 (M)	
Total fat	20 g	60 g or less (F), 70 g or less (M)	
Saturated fat	10 g	20 g or less (F), 23 g or less (M)	
Cholesterol	95 mg	300 mg or less	
Sodium	264 mg	2,400 mg or less	
Carbohydrates	46 g	250 g or more	
Protein	6 g	55 g to 90 g	

NOTES

CRANBERRY-NUT PIE

Under the swirl of pecans, cranberries add vibrant color and flavor to this deliciously different holiday pie.

Prep time: 35 minutes plus chilling
Baking time: 1 hour
O *Degree of difficulty: easy*

Fully Baked Flaky Pastry
  (recipe, page 7)
3 **large eggs**
1 **cup dark corn syrup**
⅔ **cup granulated sugar**
6 **tablespoons butter *or* margarine,**
  melted
1 **teaspoon vanilla extract**
¼ **teaspoon mace**
  Pinch salt
1 **cup fresh *or* frozen cranberries,**
  coarsely chopped
1 **cup pecan halves, toasted**

1 Prepare Fully Baked Flaky Pastry as directed. Cool completely.

2 Reduce oven temperature to 350°F. For filling, whisk the eggs in a large bowl until frothy. Whisk in the corn syrup, sugar, butter, vanilla, mace, and salt. Stir in the cranberries. Pour the filling into the baked pastry shell. Arrange the pecans on top. Bake for 50 to 60 minutes or until almost set. Cool completely on a wire rack. Makes 8 servings.

PER SERVING		DAILY GOAL
Calories	530	2,000 (F), 2,500 (M)
Total fat	27 g	60 g or less (F), 70 g or less (M)
Saturated fat	12 g	20 g or less (F), 23 g or less (M)
Cholesterol	126 mg	300 mg or less
Sodium	348 mg	2,400 mg or less
Carbohydrates	69 g	250 g or more
Protein	5 g	55 g to 90 g

RUM-PECAN PIE

Here's the classic pie that no holiday table should be without. Combine toasted walnuts and pecans if you like, but dark rum is a must.

Prep time: 25 minutes plus chilling
Baking time: 65 to 72 minutes
O *Degree of difficulty: easy*

Fully Baked Flaky Pastry
  (recipe, page 7)
2 **large eggs, lightly beaten**
⅔ **cup firmly packed brown sugar**
⅔ **cup corn syrup**
¼ **cup dark rum**
2 **tablespoons butter *or* margarine,**
  melted
2 **cups toasted pecans**

1 Prepare Fully Baked Flaky Pastry as directed. Cool Completely.

2 Reduce oven temperature to 350°F. For filling, combine the eggs, brown sugar, corn syrup, rum, and butter in a medium bowl. Fold in the pecans. Pour the filling into the baked pastry shell. Bake for 45 to 50 minutes or until just set. Cool completely on a wire rack. Makes 8 servings.

PER SERVING		DAILY GOAL
Calories	560	2,000 (F), 2,500 (M)
Total fat	34 g	60 g or less (F), 70 g or less (M)
Saturated fat	10 g	20 g or less (F), 23 g or less (M)
Cholesterol	84 mg	300 mg or less
Sodium	241 mg	2,400 mg or less
Carbohydrates	62 g	250 g or more
Protein	6 g	55 g to 90 g

NOTES

_____

_____

_____

_____

FOUR-FRUIT PIE

We used an assortment of seasonal fruits such as apples, pears, plums, and grapes—all at their peak—to make a surprising, sweet-tart filling for a double crust pie.

Prep time: 1 hour plus chilling
Baking time: 65 to 70 minutes
Degree of difficulty: moderate

Double Flaky Pastry
    (recipe, page 8)
1 **cup granulated sugar**
⅓ **cup all-purpose flour**
2 **cups peeled, sliced apples**
      (¾ pound)
2 **cups peeled, sliced pears (1 pound)**
2 **cups thinly sliced plums (1 pound)**
2 **cups halved, seedless grapes**
      (¾ pound)
1 **tablespoon fresh lemon juice**
1 **tablespoon butter *or* margarine,**
    cut up

1 Prepare Double Flaky Pastry as directed.

2 Preheat oven to 425°F. For filling, combine the sugar and flour in a large bowl. Add the apples, pears, plums, grapes, and lemon juice, tossing to combine.

3 On a lightly floured surface with a floured rolling pin, roll the larger disk into a 12-inch circle and fit into a 9-inch pie pan, leaving a 1-inch overhang. Spoon the fruit mixture into pastry shell. Dot with butter. Roll the remaining pastry into an 11-inch circle. Cut vents and place on top of filling. Trim and flute edge of pastry.

4 Place pie on a cookie sheet and bake for 15 minutes. Reduce oven temperature to 375°F. Bake for 50 to 55 minutes more or until filling is bubbly in center. (If pastry browns too quickly, cover top loosely with foil.) Cool on a wire rack 1 hour. Makes 8 servings.

PER SERVING		DAILY GOAL
Calories	510	2,000 (F), 2,500 (M)
Total fat	21 g	60 g or less (F), 70 g or less (M)
Saturated fat	10 g	20 g or less (F), 23 g or less (M)
Cholesterol	35 mg	300 mg or less
Sodium	270 mg	2,400 mg or less
Carbohydrates	81 g	250 g or more
Protein	5 g	55 g to 90 g

GOING NUTS

Nuts, which contain a great deal of oil, are highly perishable and can go rancid quickly. Purchase nuts in cans or sealed bags. Once they are opened, wrap them well and freeze them up to 6 months to retain their freshest flavor. A good rule of thumb is to always taste a nut that's been in storage before preparing your pie.

For any recipe, toasting nuts heightens their flavor. Here's how:

Oven: Preheat oven to 350°F. Spread the nuts on a baking sheet in a single layer. Bake for 8 to 10 minutes or until lightly toasted and fragrant, stirring once. Cool completely.

Microwave: Cover the bottom of your microwave oven with wax paper. Spread with ½ cup chopped nuts. Microwave, uncovered, on high (100% power) for 3 to 5 minutes or until lightly browned, stirring once.

71

PEAR-ANISE PIE

The key to a perfect pear pie is using two kinds of ripe pears for a range of flavors and juiciness. If you can get them, try fragrant Comice pears. A hint of anise adds a unique touch.

Prep time: 30 minutes plus chilling
Baking time: 65 to 75 minutes
● *Degree of difficulty: moderate*

Pastry

- 2 **cups all-purpose flour**
- ¼ **cup confectioners' sugar**
- ½ **teaspoon salt**
- ½ **cup cold butter, cut up (no substitutions)**
- ¼ **cup vegetable shortening**
- 3 **tablespoons fresh lemon juice**
- 1 **to 3 tablespoons ice water**

Filling

- ½ **cup plus 1 tablespoon granulated sugar, divided**
- ¼ **cup all-purpose flour**
- ¾ **teaspoon grated lemon peel, divided**
- ¼ **teaspoon crushed anise seed**
- 8 **cups assorted peeled, ripe pears, cut into 8 wedges each**
- 1 **large egg white, lightly beaten**
- 1 **tablespoon butter, cut up**

1 For pastry, combine the flour, confectioners' sugar, and salt in a large bowl. Gradually add the butter and shortening, tossing gently until all pieces are coated with flour. With a pastry blender or 2 knives, cut in butter and shortening until mixture resembles fine crumbs. Sprinkle with lemon juice, 1 tablespoon at a time, (then water if necessary) tossing vigorously with a fork until pastry just begins to hold together. On a smooth surface, shape the pastry into a ball, kneading lightly if necessary. Divide pastry into 2 balls, 1 slightly larger than the other. Flatten into 2 thick disks. Wrap tightly in plastic wrap and refrigerate for 30 minutes.

2 Preheat oven to 425°F. For filling, combine ½ cup of the granulated sugar, flour, ½ teaspoon of the lemon peel, and the anise seed in a large bowl. Add the pears, tossing to combine.

3 On a lightly floured surface with a floured rolling pin, roll the larger pastry disk into a 12-inch circle and fit into a 9-inch deep-dish pie pan, leaving a 1-inch overhang. Trim and flute the edge of pastry. Line pastry shell with foil and fill with dried beans or uncooked rice. Bake for 10 minutes. Remove foil and beans. Brush with some of the egg white and bake pastry for 5 minutes more.

4 Spoon pear filling into the pastry shell and dot with butter. Roll the remaining pastry disk to a 9-inch circle. Cut vents and place over filling, tucking in edges. Brush with egg white. Combine the remaining 1 tablespoon sugar with the remaining ¼ teaspoon lemon peel and sprinkle over top crust.

5 Place pie on a cookie sheet and bake for 15 minutes. Reduce oven temperature to 375°F. Bake for 50 to 60 minutes more or until the filling is bubbly in the center. (If pastry browns too quickly, cover top loosely with foil.) Cool pie on a wire rack 1 hour. Makes 8 servings.

PER SERVING		DAILY GOAL
Calories	470	2,000 (F), 2,500 (M)
Total fat	20 g	60 g or less (F), 70 g or less (M)
Saturated fat	10 g	20 g or less (F), 23 g or less (M)
Cholesterol	35 mg	300 mg or less
Sodium	276 mg	2,400 mg or less
Carbohydrates	70 g	250 g or more
Protein	5 g	55 g to 90 g

CRANBERRY-PEAR PIE

We cut the top pastry crust into decorative wedges to allow all the beautiful ruby-red fruit filling to shine through. Use ripe Comice or Bartlett pears.

Prep time: 50 minutes plus chilling
Baking time: 65 to 70 minutes
Degree of difficulty: moderate

Double Flaky Pastry
(recipe, page 8)
⅔ **cup granulated sugar**
Water
3 **pounds ripe pears, peeled, cored, and diced**
1½ **cups fresh or frozen cranberries**
½ **teaspoon grated lemon peel**
¼ **teaspoon salt**
3 **tablespoons cornstarch**
1 **tablespoon butter or margarine**
½ **teaspoon vanilla extract**

1 Prepare Double Flaky Pastry as directed.

2 For filling, combine the sugar and ½ cup water in a large saucepan; bring to a boil. Reduce heat and simmer for 5 minutes. Add the pears, cranberries, lemon peel, and salt. Simmer about 10 minutes or until the cranberries have popped, stirring occasionally. Dissolve the cornstarch in ¼ cup water in a small bowl. Stir cornstarch mixture into the cranberry mixture; bring to a boil. Reduce heat and simmer for 2 minutes, stirring occasionally. Remove from heat and stir in the butter and vanilla. Cool completely.

3 Preheat oven to 425°F. On a lightly floured surface with a floured rolling pin, roll the larger pastry disk into a 12-inch circle and fit into a 9½-inch deep-dish pie pan. With a knife or fluted pastry cutter, trim pastry to edge of pan. Pour the pear-cranberry mixture into the pastry shell.

4 Roll the remaining pastry into an 11-inch circle, then trim with a small sharp knife to a 10-inch circle. Cut into 8 equal wedges. Place wedges, overlapping, on top of filling. With the tines of a fork, press pastry edge to seal.

5 Bake for 15 minutes. Reduce oven temperature to 375°F. Bake for 50 to 55 minutes more or until the pears are tender and the filling is bubbly. (If pastry browns too quickly, cover top loosely with foil.) Cool completely on wire rack or serve warm. Makes 8 servings.

PER SERVING		DAILY GOAL
Calories	465	2,000 (F), 2,500 (M)
Total fat	20 g	60 g or less (F), 70 g or less (M)
Saturated fat	10 g	20 g or less (F), 23 g or less (M)
Cholesterol	35 mg	300 mg or less
Sodium	337 mg	2,400 mg or less
Carbohydrates	70 g	250 g or more
Protein	4 g	55 g to 90 g

CRAZY FOR CRANBERRIES

The peak season for fresh cranberries is October through December. For cranberries all year long, tightly wrap fresh cranberries and refrigerate up to 1 month or freeze up to 1 year. When selecting cranberries, look for firm, bright red berries and discard any shriveled or white cranberries. Unthawed frozen cranberries can be used interchangeably with the fresh berries in any of these holiday pies.

CHOCOLATE-PECAN TART

At the Inn at Little Washington in Virginia (the only inn to earn five stars in the Mobil Travel Guide), the pairing of pecans and chocolate in this luscious tart, makes it one of the inn's most popular and delectable desserts.

Prep time: 1 hour plus chilling
Baking time: 46 to 48 minutes
● *Degree of difficulty: moderate*

1   **10-inch Ultimate Tart Pastry shell (recipe, page 9)**
2   **squares (2 ounces) semisweet chocolate, melted**

Filling

1⅓   **cups granulated sugar**
⅓   **cup water**
1   **cup heavy *or* whipping cream**
¼   **cup butter, cut up**
1   **large egg, lightly beaten**
1   **cup pecans, toasted and chopped**

Chocolate Wedges
3   **squares (3 ounces) semisweet chocolate, melted**
Whipped cream, for garnish

1   Prepare a 10-inch Ultimate Tart Pastry shell as directed. Cool completely.

2   Reduce oven temperature to 400°F. Brush the bottom of the cooled pastry shell with melted chocolate. Place the tart pan with pastry shell on a cookie sheet.

3   For filling, combine the sugar and water in a medium, heavy-bottomed saucepan. Bring to a boil over medium heat and boil about 15 minutes or until amber-colored and sugar is dissolved. *(Do not stir.)* Remove from heat and gradually whisk in the heavy cream until smooth. Add the butter and whisk until melted, then whisk in the egg. Stir in the pecans.

4   Carefully pour filling into the prepared pastry shell. Bake for 10 minutes. Reduce oven temperature to 350°F. Bake for 10 minutes more or until the filling is bubbly in the center. Cool completely on a wire rack. (Can be made ahead. Cover and refrigerate up to 24 hours.)

5   For Chocolate Wedges, trace the outline of a 10-inch tart pan onto wax paper. Cut wax paper circle into 8 wedges. Place wedges on another sheet of wax paper. Pipe melted chocolate along edge of 1 wedge, then fill in outline with a free-form lacy pattern. Repeat with remaining wedges. Refrigerate until set. Serve tart with whipped cream and Chocolate Wedges. Makes 8 servings.

PER SLICE WITH 1 CHOCOLATE WEDGE		DAILY GOAL
Calories	590	2,000 (F), 2,500 (M)
Total fat	41 g	60 g or less (F), 70 g or less (M)
Saturated fat	20 g	20 g or less (F), 23 g or less (M)
Cholesterol	103 mg	300 mg or less
Sodium	173 mg	2,400 mg or less
Carbohydrates	59 g	250 g or more
Protein	5 g	55 g to 90 g

NOTES

_____

_____

_____

_____

_____

_____

FROZEN PUMPKIN MOUSSE PIE

Whipped cream is folded into pumpkin purée and seasoned with ginger and nutmeg. Because the pie is frozen, it works well to make it ahead. Wrap the pie well and freeze it for up to 4 days.

Prep time: 20 minutes plus cooling and freezing
Baking time: 8 minutes
○ *Degree of difficulty: easy*

Crust
1¼ cups graham cracker crumbs
¼ cup granulated sugar
5 tablespoons butter *or* margarine, melted

Filling
1 can (16 ounces) solid-pack pumpkin
¾ cup granulated sugar
½ teaspoon ginger
¼ teaspoon nutmeg
¼ teaspoon salt
1½ cups heavy *or* whipping cream, divided
¼ cup confectioners' sugar

1 Preheat oven to 375°F. For crust, combine the cracker crumbs, sugar, and melted butter in a small bowl. Pat mixture evenly onto bottom and sides of a 9-inch pie pan. Bake for 8 minutes or until golden brown. Cool completely on a wire rack.

2 Meanwhile, for filling, heat the pumpkin, sugar, ginger, nutmeg, and salt in a medium saucepan, stirring constantly, about 4 minutes or until sugar is melted. Remove from heat; cool.

3 Beat 1 cup of the cream in a mixing bowl until stiff. Fold into cooled pumpkin mixture with a rubber spatula. Spoon into prepared crust. Wrap lightly with plastic wrap and freeze about 8 hours or until firm.

4 One hour before serving, remove the pie from the freezer and let stand at room temperature. Just before serving, beat the remaining ½ cup cream with confectioners' sugar until stiff. Spread whipped cream evenly over the pie. Makes 12 servings.

PER SERVING		DAILY GOAL
Calories	280	2,000 (F), 2,500 (M)
Total fat at	17 g	60 g or less (F), 70 g or less (M)
Saturated fat	10 g	20 g or less (F), 23 g or less (M)
Cholesterol	54 mg	300 mg or less
Sodium	182 mg	2,400 mg or less
Carbohydrates	32 g	250 g or more
Protein	2 g	55 g to 90 g

CARAMELIZED UPSIDE-DOWN PEAR TART WITH CRANBERRIES

Here's our interpretation of the classic French fruit dessert Tart Tatin, tailor-made for Thanksgiving.

Prep time: 55 minutes plus chilling
Baking time: 35 to 40 minutes
● *Degree of difficulty: moderate*

Ultimate Tart Pastry (recipe, page 9)
½ cup dried cranberries
¼ cup Armagnac *or* brandy
3 tablespoons butter (no substitutions)
8 firm Bosc pears (3½ pounds), peeled, quartered and cored

½ **cup granulated sugar**

½ **cup crème fraîche *or* sour cream**

1 Prepare Ultimate Tart Pastry as directed, except on a lightly floured surface with a lightly floured rolling pin, roll pastry to a 10-inch circle. Transfer to a cookie sheet lined with waxed paper and refrigerate. (*Do not follow steps 2, 3, or 4.*)

2 Meanwhile, heat the cranberries and Armagnac in a small saucepan just until boiling. Remove from heat. Cover and let stand for 20 to 30 minutes, stirring occasionally. Drain.

3 Preheat oven to 425°F. Melt the butter in a deep 12-inch skillet over medium-high heat. Add the pears and sugar and cook, stirring occasionally to prevent sticking, for 20 minutes. Increase the heat to high and cook for 15 to 20 minutes more or until the pears are deep, golden brown. Stir in the cranberries. Spoon mixture into a 9-inch glass pie plate.

4 Place pastry circle over pear-cranberry mixture, tucking in dough around edges. Place tart on a cookie sheet. Bake for 35 to 40 minutes or until pastry is golden

brown. Immediately invert tart onto a large, heat-proof platter. Serve warm or at room temperature with crème fraîche. Makes 8 servings.

PER SERVING		DAILY GOAL
Calories	420	2,000 (F), 2,500 (M)
Total fat	20 g	60 g or less (F), 70 g or less (M)
Saturated fat	12 g	20 g or less (F), 23 g or less (M)
Cholesterol	49 mg	300 mg or less
Sodium	88 mg	2,400 mg or less
Carbohydrates	61 g	250 g or more
Protein	3 g	55 g to 90 g

BRANDIED CUSTARD SAUCE

This sauce is simply divine with any winter fruit pie or tart.

Prep time: 5 minutes plus chilling
Cooking time: 10 minutes
○ *Degree of difficulty: easy*

1 cup heavy *or* whipping cream
1 cup milk
3 tablespoons granulated sugar
4 large egg yolks
2 tablespoons brandy
1 teaspoon vanilla extract

1 Combine the cream, milk, and sugar in a medium saucepan and heat to scalding.

2 Meanwhile, whisk the egg yolks in a medium bowl until lemon-colored. Gradually pour hot cream mixture into egg yolks, whisking constantly. Return to saucepan, then cook over low heat, stirring constantly, until thick enough to coat the back of a spoon. Remove from heat. Stir in the brandy and vanilla. Refrigerate about 2 hours or until cold. Makes 2 cups.

PER TABLESPOON		DAILY GOAL
Calories	45	2,000 (F), 2,500 (M)
Total fat	3 g	60 g or less (F), 70 g or less (M)
Saturated fat	2 g	20 g or less (F), 23 g or less (M)
Cholesterol	38 mg	300 mg or less
Sodium	7 mg	2,400 mg or less
Carbohydrates	2 g	250 g or more
Protein	1 g	55 g to 90 g

A PASSION FOR PEARS

Bartlett, Anjou, Comice, and the firm-textured Bosc are great baked in pies and tarts. Choose pears with a smooth skin, spicy fragrance, and juicy interior.

CRANBERRY-ORANGE-GOAT CHEESE TART

Under a beautiful cranberry crown, the addition of mild goat cheese lends just the right amount of tartness to this creamy tart filling spiked with orange. *Also pictured on page 64.*

Prep time: 45 minutes plus chilling
Baking time: 30 to 35 minutes
Degree of difficulty: moderate

Ultimate Tart Pastry (recipe, page 9)

Filling

- ¼ **cup unsalted butter, softened (no substitutions)**
- ½ **cup granulated sugar**
- 2 **packages (3 ounces each) cream cheese, softened**
- 4 **ounces mild goat cheese, softened**
- 1 **teaspoon vanilla extract**
- ½ **teaspoon grated orange peel**
- 2 **large eggs**

Topping

- ⅔ **cup granulated sugar**
- 8 **tablespoons water, divided**
- 1½ **cups fresh *or* frozen cranberries**
- ¼ **teaspoon grated orange peel**
- 4 **teaspoons cornstarch**
  Orange slices, for garnish

1 Preheat oven to 425°F. Prepare Ultimate Tart Pastry as directed, except bake for 10 minutes. Remove the foil and beans and bake pastry for 12 minutes more or until golden. Cool completely on wire rack. Reduce oven temperature to 375°F.

2 For filling, beat the butter and sugar in a large mixing bowl until light and fluffy. Beat in the cream cheese, goat cheese, vanilla, and orange peel until smooth. With mixer at low speed, beat in the eggs, 1 at a time, until blended. Pour into baked pastry shell. Bake for 30 to 35 minutes or until a wooden toothpick inserted in center comes out clean. Cool on a wire rack.

3 Meanwhile, for topping, combine the sugar and 6 tablespoons of the water in a medium saucepan; bring to a boil. Reduce heat and simmer for 5 minutes. Add the cranberries and orange peel. Simmer for 5 minutes or until cranberries pop. Dissolve the cornstarch in the remaining 2 tablespoons water in a small bowl. Stir cornstarch mixture into cranberry mixture; bring to a boil. Reduce heat and simmer for 2 minutes. Remove from heat and cool completely.

4 Spoon the cranberry topping over tart. Refrigerate at least 4 hours or overnight. Remove from tart pan and garnish with orange slices. Makes 8 servings.

PER SERVING		DAILY GOAL
Calories	470	2,000 (F), 2,500 (M)
Total fat	20 g	60 g or less (F), 70 g or less (M)
Saturated fat	10 g	20 g or less (F), 23 g or less (M)
Cholesterol	35 mg	300 mg or less
Sodium	276 mg	2,400 mg or less
Carbohydrates	70 g	250 g or more
Protein	5 g	55 g to 90 g

NOTES

_____

_____

_____

_____

_____

_____

_____

MAPLE-BUTTERNUT TART WITH GLAZED PECANS

This fall tart is an elegant alternative to the usual pumpkin pie. Either fresh or frozen squash can be used, but real maple syrup makes all the difference.

Ⓜ *Microwave*
   Prep time: 30 minutes plus chilling
   Baking time: 45 to 53 minutes
◑ *Degree of difficulty: moderate*

**Ultimate Tart Pastry
   (recipe, page 9)**
1¼ **pounds butternut squash, peeled
      and diced in ½-inch pieces, *or*
      1 package (10 ounces) frozen
      winter squash purée, thawed**
  2 **teaspoons butter, melted**
  ⅓ **cup plus 2 tablespoons pure maple
      syrup**
 16 **pecan halves**
  1 **large egg white, lightly beaten**
  ⅓ **cup heavy *or* whipping cream**
  2 **tablespoons granulated sugar**
  2 **large eggs, lightly beaten**
  ⅛ **teaspoon nutmeg**

Maple Whipped Cream
  ⅔ **cup heavy *or* whipping cream**
  2 **tablespoons pure maple syrup**

1 Prepare Ultimate Tart Pastry through Steps 1 and 2 as directed, except do not prick dough. *(Do not follow steps 3 and 4.)*

2 Meanwhile, preheat oven to 375°F. Bake squash in a covered baking dish about 30 minutes or until very tender. Or, microwave in a shallow, 2-quart microwave-proof dish on high (100% power) for 15 minutes or until very tender. Press through a sieve into a medium bowl.

3 Combine the butter, 2 tablespoons of the maple syrup and the pecans in a pie plate. Bake for 10 minutes. Cool in pie plate on a wire rack, turning nuts occasionally to coat.

4 Line the frozen pastry shell with foil and fill with dried beans or uncooked rice. Bake for 10 minutes. Remove foil and beans. Brush the inside of the pastry with egg white and bake for 5 to 8 minutes

more or until golden. Cool completely on wire rack.

5 Reduce oven temperature to 350°F. Whisk the ⅓ cup maple syrup, the cream, sugar, eggs, and nutmeg into squash. Place tart pan on a cookie sheet on the oven rack and carefully pour squash mixture into baked pastry shell. Bake for 20 minutes. Remove tart from oven and arrange the glazed pecans around edge. Return to oven and bake for 10 to 15 minutes more or until filling is just set. Cool completely on a wire rack. Makes 8 servings.

6 For Maple Whipped Cream, beat the cream to stiff peaks in a small mixing bowl. Beat in the maple syrup. Serve with cooled tart.

PER SERVING WITH WHIPPED CREAM		DAILY GOAL
Calories	415	2,000 (F), 2,500 (M)
Total fat	26 g	60 g or less (F), 70 g or less (M)
Saturated fat	15 g	20 g or less (F), 23 g or less (M)
Cholesterol	127 mg	300 mg or less
Sodium	85 mg	2,400 mg or less
Carbohydrates	42 g	250 g or more
Protein	5 g	55 g to 90 g

HOLIDAY FIGGY TART

This extra-large dried fruit tart is an elegant substitute for the traditional fruit cake. It can be baked ahead, wrapped well, and frozen. Simply thaw it overnight at room temperature before serving.

Prep time: 35 minutes plus chilling
Baking time: 53 to 55 minutes
Degree of difficulty: moderate

Single Flaky Pastry (recipe, page 7)
1   cup dried Calimyrna figs, coarsely chopped
1   cup dried cranberries
½   cup golden raisins
¾   cup fresh orange juice
½   cup light corn syrup
¼   cup firmly packed brown sugar
2   tablespoons butter *or* margarine, melted
1   teaspoon grated orange peel
¼   teaspoon cinnamon
3   large eggs
¼   teaspoon salt
1   cup walnuts, coarsely chopped
¼   cup apple *or* red currant jelly, melted

1   Prepare Single Flaky Pastry crust as directed through Step 1. *(Do not follow step 2.)*

2   Place the figs, cranberries, and raisins in a small bowl. Bring the orange juice to a boil in a small saucepan and pour over dried fruit. Let stand for 1 hour, stirring occasionally.

3   Preheat oven to 425°F. On a lightly floured surface with a floured rolling pin, roll pastry into a 16-inch circle. Fold pastry in half. Carefully transfer to a 12-inch tart pan with a removable bottom. Gently press pastry with fingertips along bottom and up side of pan. With scissors, trim pastry to 1 inch above edge. Fold overhanging pastry into side of crust and gently press edge up to extend ¼ inch above side of pan.

4   Line pastry shell with foil and fill with dried beans or uncooked rice. Bake for 15 minutes. Remove foil and beans and prick pastry all over with a fork. Bake for 8 to 10 minutes more or until golden. Cool slightly on wire rack. Reduce oven temperature to 375°F.

5   Whisk the corn syrup, brown sugar, butter, orange peel, cinnamon, eggs, and salt together in a large bowl. Stir in dried fruit mixture and walnuts. Spoon into baked pastry. Bake for 30 minutes. Cool completely on a wire rack. Brush hot jelly over tart and let stand until glaze sets. Makes 16 servings.

PER SERVING		DAILY GOAL
Calories	295	2,000 (F), 2,500 (M)
Total fat at	13 g	60 g or less (F), 70 g or less (M)
Saturated fat	5 g	20 g or less (F), 23 g or less (M)
Cholesterol	55 mg	300 mg or less
Sodium	157 mg	2,400 mg or less
Carbohydrates	44 g	250 g or more
Protein	4 g	55 g to 90 g

NOTES

_____

_____

_____

_____

_____

_____

_____

_____

FRUITED MINCEMEAT TART

This spicy, all-fruit filling, which features both fresh and dried fruits, is even better if prepared a day ahead. The tart can also be baked, then cooled and frozen up to 2 weeks.

Prep time: 75 minutes plus chilling
Baking time: 55 to 60 minutes
● *Degree of difficulty: moderate*

Pastry

1½	cups all-purpose flour
1½	teaspoons granulated sugar
½	teaspoon salt
½	cup cold butter, cut up
4	to 6 tablespoons ice water

Filling

2	pears (about 1 pound) peeled, cored and diced
2	Golden Delicious apples (about 1 pound), peeled, cored and diced
1	cup water
⅓	cup chopped dried figs
⅓	cup chopped pitted prunes
⅓	cup firmly packed brown sugar
¼	cup chopped dried apricots
¼	cup golden raisins
2	tablespoons fresh lemon juice
¼	teaspoon grated lemon peel
¼	teaspoon cinnamon
	Pinch nutmeg
	Pinch ginger
	Pinch allspice
1½	cups chopped walnuts, toasted
3	tablespoons brandy
	Brandied Custard Sauce (recipe, page 77) (optional)

1 For pastry, combine the flour, sugar, and salt in a medium bowl. Gradually add the butter, tossing gently until all pieces are coated with flour. With a pastry blender or 2 knives, cut in butter until mixture resembles coarse crumbs. Sprinkle with ice water, 1 tablespoon at a time, tossing vigorously with a fork until pastry just begins to hold together. On a smooth surface, shape pastry into a ball, kneading lightly if necessary. Divide pastry into 2 balls, 1 slightly larger than the other. Flatten into 2 thick disks. Wrap tightly in plastic wrap and refrigerate 1 hour or overnight.

2 For filling, combine the pears, apples, water, figs, prunes, brown sugar, apricots, raisins, lemon juice, lemon peel, cinnamon, nutmeg, ginger, and allspice in a large saucepan. Bring to a boil. Reduce heat and simmer, stirring occasionally, for 35 to 40 minutes or until fruits are tender and filling is thickened. Remove from heat. Stir in walnuts and brandy. Cool.

3 Preheat oven to 425°F. On a lightly floured surface with a floured rolling pin, roll larger disk into an 11-inch circle and fit into a 9½-inch tart pan with a removable bottom, leaving a ½-inch overhang. Spoon filling into pastry shell. Roll remaining pastry into a 9½-inch circle. Using a fluted pastry cutter, cut into ten ½-inch-wide strips and arrange in a lattice pattern on top of fruit. Fold overhang up over strips; trim to edge.

4 Bake for 10 minutes. Reduce oven temperature to 375°F. Bake for 45 to 50 minutes more or until the filling is bubbly and crust is golden. Cool completely on a wire rack. Serve with Brandied Custard Sauce, if desired. Makes 8 servings.

PER SERVING WITHOUT SAUCE		DAILY GOAL
Calories	515	2,000 (F), 2,500 (M)
Total fat	26 g	60 g or less (F), 70 g or less (M)
Saturated fat	8 g	20 g or less (F), 23 g or less (M)
Cholesterol	31 mg	300 mg or less
Sodium	262 mg	2,400 mg or less
Carbohydrates	63 g	250 g or more
Protein	7 g	55 g to 90 g

MCINTOSH APPLE TART

This delectable dessert should be made no earlier than Thanksgiving morning. No need to serve it with whipped cream—it's already in the filling.

Prep time: 1 hour plus chilling
Baking time: 70 minutes
● *Degree of difficulty: moderate*

Ultimate Tart Pastry
(recipe, page 9)
Filling
- ¾ **cup sugar, divided**
- 2 **tablespoons all-purpose flour**
- 1 **teaspoon cinnamon**
- ¼ **teaspoon nutmeg**
- 3 **pounds McIntosh *or* Golden Delicious apples, peeled, cored, and sliced ¼-inch thick**
- ½ **cup heavy *or* whipping cream**

1 Prepare Ultimate Tart Pastry as directed through Steps 1 and 2, except use an 11-inch tart pan and do not prick dough. Refrigerate while preparing the filling. *(Do not follow steps 3 and 4.)*

2 Preheat oven to 350°F. For filling, combine ½ cup of the sugar, flour, cinnamon, and nutmeg in a large bowl. Add the apples, tossing to coat.

3 At edge of prepared tart shell, arrange the apple slices, slightly overlapping, in a circle. Make another circle inside it and continue until the tart shell is completely covered. Top with another layer of apples.

4 Bake tart for 1 hour. Carefully pour the cream over the apples and sprinkle with the remaining ¼ cup sugar. Bake for 10 minutes more or until the apples are tender and crust is golden. Cool on a wire rack. Makes 12 servings.

PER SERVING		DAILY GOAL
Calories	260	2,000 (F), 2,500 (M)
Total fat	12 g	60 g or less (F), 70 g or less (M)
Saturated fat	7 g	20 g or less (F), 23 g or less (M)
Cholesterol	34 mg	300 mg or less
Sodium	28 mg	2,400 mg or less
Carbohydrates	38 g	250 g or more
Protein	2 g	55 g to 90 g

PEAR TART WITH FRANGIPANE CREAM

Here's a stunning dessert from Alice Waters, owner of Chez Panisse restaurant in California. She suggests rooting around your local farmers' markets for unusual pears for the filling. Buttery pears, such as Anjou or Bosc, add rich flavor to this tart.

Prep time: 30 minutes plus cooling and chilling
Cooking time: 50 minutes
● *Degree of difficulty: moderate*

Pastry
- 1 **cup all-purpose flour**
- 1 **tablespoon granulated sugar**
- ¼ **teaspoon salt**
- ¼ **teaspoon grated lemon peel**
- ½ **cup unsalted butter, softened and cut up (no substitutions)**
- 1 **tablespoon water**
- ½ **teaspoon vanilla extract**

Frangipane Cream
- 1 **cup milk**
- 3 **tablespoons granulated sugar**
- 2 **tablespoons all-purpose flour**

3 large egg yolks
1 tablespoon unsalted butter
2 tablespoons crushed amaretti
   cookies
½ teaspoon kirsch

Filling
2¼ cups water
¾   cup granulated sugar
1   piece (2 inches) vanilla bean, split
    or 1½ teaspoons vanilla extract
1½ pounds firm, ripe, buttery pears
    (Anjou or Bosc), peeled, cored,
    and quartered
2   tablespoons apricot jam
¼   teaspoon kirsch
1   tablespoon finely chopped
    pistachios

1 For pastry, combine the flour, sugar, salt, and lemon peel in a medium bowl. Gradually add the butter, 1 piece at a time, tossing gently until all pieces are coated with flour. With a pastry blender or 2 knives, cut in butter until mixture resembles fine crumbs. Combine the water and vanilla, then add to pastry, tossing vigorously with a fork until pastry just begins to hold together. On a smooth surface, shape pastry into a ball, kneading lightly if necessary. Flatten into a thick disk. Wrap tightly in plastic wrap and refrigerate 30 minutes.

2 On a lightly floured surface with a floured rolling pin, roll pastry into an 11-inch circle. Fold pastry in half. Carefully transfer to a 9- to 9½-inch tart pan with a removable bottom. Gently press pastry with fingertips along bottom and up side of pan. Cover and freeze for 30 minutes or refrigerate overnight.

3 Preheat oven to 375°F. Bake pastry for 25 minutes or until golden. Cool completely on wire rack.

4 For Frangipane Cream, bring milk just to a boil in a small saucepan. Combine the sugar and flour in a heavy medium saucepan. Gradually whisk in hot milk. Bring to a boil over medium heat, then boil, stirring constantly, 2 minutes. Whisk the egg yolks in a small bowl until light. Gradually whisk half the milk mixture into the eggs. Return mixture to the saucepan and cook, stirring constantly, for 4 to 5 minutes or until very thick. *(Do not boil.)* Remove from heat and stir in butter. Strain through a sieve, then stir in the amaretti crumbs and kirsch. Cover with plastic wrap and refrigerate until cold.

5 For filling, heat the water, sugar, and vanilla bean to boiling in a large saucepan over medium heat. Add the pears to the hot syrup, then cover and simmer about 15 minutes or until just tender. Remove pears from syrup. (Can be made ahead. Cover and refrigerate pears up to 24 hours. Reserve syrup to add to fresh fruits.)

6 To assemble, spread Frangipane Cream in bottom of baked tart shell. Pat pears dry on paper towels and slice lengthwise ¼-inch thick. Arrange slices in tart shell, overlapping halfway, beginning at outside edge of tart. Heat the jam in small saucepan until bubbly. Stir in the kirsch and brush over pears. Sprinkle with pistachios. Serve within 3 to 4 hours. Makes 8 servings.

PER SERVING		DAILY GOAL
Calories	340	2,000 (F), 2,500 (M)
Total fat	17 g	60 g or less (F), 70 g or less (M)
Saturated fat	9 g	20 g or less (F), 23 g or less (M)
Cholesterol	119 mg	300 mg or less
Sodium	89 mg	2,400 mg or less
Carbohydrates	44 g	250 g or more
Protein	5 g	55 g to 90 g

OUR MOST

ELEGANT TARTS

Fruit-studded and creamy, rich fillings nestled in tender pastry—tarts are the most elegant and impressive of open-faced pies. Surprise your guests with choices like our beautiful Double Raspberry Tart with raspberry curd, individual Crème Brûlèe Tartlets with caramelized sugar, or a glorious lattice-topped Black Raspberry Linzer Torte. Whatever the choice, a tart is sure to please.

DOUBLE RASPBERRY TART

We doubled the raspberry by spreading purée on the baked crust and topping it with whole berries.

Ⓜ *Microwave*
   Prep time: 20 minutes plus chilling
   Baking time: 26 to 28 minutes
⬤ *Degree of difficulty: moderate*

1   **10-inch Ultimate Tart Pastry (recipe, page 9)**

Filling

3   **cups fresh raspberries, divided**
½   **cup granulated sugar**
1   **teaspoon cornstarch**
2   **tablespoons butter, cut up (no substitutions)**
     Sweetened whipped cream, for garnish (optional)

1 Prepare Ultimate Tart Pastry as directed.

2 For filling, purée 1 cup of the raspberries in a food processor or blender. Strain through a wire mesh strainer set over a 2-cup microwave-proof glass measure, discarding seeds. Stir the sugar and cornstarch into purée, then add the butter. Cover with plastic wrap, turning back a section to vent. Microwave on high (100% power) for 2 minutes or until mixture is thickened. Whisk until smooth.

3 Spread purée evenly over baked crust. Top with the remaining 2 cups of raspberries in a single layer. Refrigerate at least 1 hour or overnight. Garnish with sweetened whipped cream, if desired. Makes 8 servings.

PER SERVING WITHOUT WHIPPED CREAM		DAILY GOAL
Calories	270	2,000 (F), 2,500 (M)
Total fat	15 g	60 g or less (F), 70 g or less (M)
Saturated fat	9 g	20 g or less (F), 23 g or less (M)
Cholesterol	39 mg	300 mg or less
Sodium	66 mg	2,400 mg or less
Carbohydrates	33 g	250 g or more
Protein	2 g	55 g to 90 g

NOTES

STRAWBERRY-ALMOND TART

Blanching almonds means removing the skins from the nuts. Place almonds in a bowl; pour boiling water over them and let stand 1 minute. Drain, then transfer the nuts to a clean, dry towel and rub to remove skins. After blanching, toast nuts in a skillet over medium-low heat, or in a 350°F. oven about 10 minutes.

Ⓜ *Microwave*
Prep time: 30 plus chilling
Baking time: 41 to 43 minutes
◕ *Degree of difficulty: moderate*

1 **9-inch Ultimate Tart Pastry**
(recipe, page 9)

Filling
¾ **cup whole blanched almonds**
⅓ **cup granulated sugar**
2 **tablespoons all-purpose flour**
¼ **cup unsalted butter, softened**
(no substitutions)
1 **large egg**

½ **teaspoon almond extract**
½ **cup strawberry preserves**
3 **tablespoons sliced blanched**
almonds, toasted
Mint sprigs, for garnish

1 Prepare Ultimate Tart Pastry as directed, except do not prick dough.

2 Reduce oven temperature to 375°F. For filling, combine the almonds, sugar, and flour in a food processor and process until finely ground. Add the butter and blend until incorporated. Add the egg and almond extract and blend until smooth.

3 Spread the filling into baked pastry shell. Bake for 15 minutes or until filling is golden. Cool completely on a wire rack. Microwave preserves in a microwave-proof glass measure on high (100% power) for 1 minute. Brush preserves over filling and sprinkle with sliced almonds. Garnish with mint. Makes 10 servings.

PER SERVING		DAILY GOAL
Calories	330	2,000 (F), 2,500 (M)
Total fat	21 g	60 g or less (F), 70 g or less (M)
Saturated fat	9 g	20 g or less (F), 23 g or less (M)
Cholesterol	58 mg	300 mg or less
Sodium	44 mg	2,400 mg or less
Carbohydrates	32 g	250 g or more
Protein	5 g	55 g to 90 g

MAINE BLUEBERRY TART

An almond-scented cookie crust holds this double blueberry filling. After a third of the berries are cooked for a rich jam-like flavor, the remaining raw berries are folded in for crunch and freshness.

Prep time: 30 minutes plus standing
Baking time: 8 minutes
O *Degree of difficulty: easy*

Crust

- 4 **cups vanilla wafer cookies**
- ¼ **cup crumbled amaretti cookies (optional)**
- 6 **tablespoons butter *or* margarine, melted**

Filling

- 6 **cups fresh blueberries, divided**
- ¾ **cup granulated sugar**
  Water
- 2 **tablespoons cornstarch**
- 1 **tablespoon butter *or* margarine**
- 1 **tablespoon fresh lemon juice**
  Unsweetened whipped cream (optional)

1 Preheat oven to 350°F. For crust, combine both kinds of cookies in a food processor and process to fine crumbs. Transfer to a large bowl and stir in the butter. Press evenly into an 11½-inch tart pan with a removable bottom. Bake 8 minutes, just until beginning to brown. Cool on a wire rack.

2 For filling, combine 2 cups of the blueberries, sugar, and 2 tablespoons water in a large saucepan. Bring to a full boil, stirring occasionally. Dissolve the cornstarch in ¼ cup water in a cup, then stir into berries in pan. Return to a full boil, stirring constantly. Reduce heat to low and cook, stirring, 2 minutes more. Remove from heat. Stir in the butter and lemon juice.

3 Gently stir in remaining 4 cups berries. Spoon filling evenly in prepared crust. Let stand 3 hours until set. Serve with whipped cream, if desired. Makes 8 servings.

PER SERVING WITHOUT WHIPPED CREAM		DAILY GOAL
Calories	405	2,000 (F), 2,500 (M)
Total fat	17 g	60 g or less (F), 70 g or less (M)
Saturated fat	8 g	20 g or less (F), 23 g or less (M)
Cholesterol	27 mg	300 mg or less
Sodium	234 mg	2,400 mg or less
Carbohydrates	66 g	250 g or more
Protein	3 g	55 g to 90 g

NOTES

BERRY'S LAST JAM TART

This tart celebrates the abundance of summer berries. To add an elegant note, stir a tablespoon of fruit liqueur or dark rum instead of vanilla into the Sweetened Whipped Cream.

Ⓜ *Microwave*
  Prep time: 20 minutes
  Baking time: 26 to 28 minutes
⊖ *Degree of difficulty: moderate*

1 **9- *or* 10-inch Ultimate Tart Pastry (recipe, page 9)**

Filling
¼ **cup strawberry, raspberry, apricot, peach *or* cherry preserves**
3 **cups mixed fresh raspberries, blueberries, blackberries, *and/or* strawberries**

Sweetened Whipped Cream
¾ **cup heavy *or* whipping cream**
1 **tablespoon confectioners' sugar**
½ **teaspoon vanilla extract**

1 Prepare Ultimate Tart Pastry as directed.

2 Microwave preserves in a microwave-proof glass-measure on high (100% power) for 30 seconds. Spread preserves over bottom of baked pastry shell. Sprinkle with assorted berries.

3 For Sweetened Whipped Cream, beat the cream and sugar to soft peaks in a small mixing bowl. Beat in the vanilla. Decorate tart with whipped cream or serve along side. Makes 8 servings.

PER SERVING		DAILY GOAL
Calories	295	2,000 (F), 2,500 (M)
Total fat	20 g	60 g or less (F), 70 g or less (M)
Saturated fat	12 g	20 g or less (F), 23 g or less (M)
Cholesterol	62 mg	300 mg or less
Sodium	47 mg	2,400 mg or less
Carbohydrates	26 g	250 g or more
Protein	3 g	55 g to 90 g

NOTES

BLACK RASPBERRY LINZER TORTE

This beautiful tart is a winning dessert from Barbara Dickinson of East Greenwich, Rhode Island, who was featured in our story "The Best Cook in Town."

Prep time: 1 hour plus chilling
Baking time: 1 hour
● *Degree of difficulty: moderate*

- ¾ **pound hazelnuts**
- 1 **cup granulated sugar**
- ¼ **teaspoon salt**
- 1 **cup unsalted butter, cut up (no substitutions)**
- 2 **large egg yolks, lightly beaten**
- 2 **teaspoons grated lemon peel**
- 1 **teaspoon vanilla extract**
- 2 **cups all-purpose flour**
- ½ **teaspoon cinnamon**
- ¼ **teaspoon freshly grated nutmeg**
  Pinch cloves
- 2 **jars (10 *or* 12 ounces each) premium-quality black raspberry *or* black currant preserves (2 cups total)**

- 1 **large egg white**
- 1 **teaspoon water**
  Confectioners' sugar

1 Preheat oven to 350°F. For crust, spread the hazelnuts on a baking sheet in a single layer. Bake for 12 to 15 minutes or until lightly browned and skins are crackly. Wrap nuts in a clean kitchen towel and let stand for 5 minutes. Rub the nuts in the towel to remove skins, then cool completely. Transfer hazelnuts to a food processor and process until finely ground. (You should have 2½ cups.)

2 Combine the sugar and salt in a large bowl. With a pastry blender or 2 knives, cut in the butter until mixture resembles coarse crumbs. Stir in the yolks, lemon peel, and vanilla. Combine ground hazelnuts, flour, cinnamon, nutmeg, and cloves in another bowl. With a pastry blender, cut nut-flour mixture into butter mixture, 1 cup at a time, until just blended after each addition and pastry is crumbly. Pat 3 cups crumbs onto bottom and side of a 12-inch tart pan with a removable bottom. Shape remaining pastry into a ball, then flatten into a thick disk. Cover and chill pastry shell and disk 2 hours or overnight.

3 Fill pastry shell with an even layer of preserves. Refrigerate.

4 Preheat oven to 400°F. Roll remaining pastry disk between 2 sheets of lightly floured wax paper into a 14-inch circle. Cut circle into ½-inch-wide strips. Freeze about 15 minutes or until firm. Carefully arrange strips on preserves 1 inch apart in a lattice pattern; trim edges. Lightly beat the egg white and water in a small bowl; brush on lattice.

5 Place torte on a cookie sheet and bake for 15 minutes. Reduce oven temperature to 350°F. Bake for 25 minutes more or until pastry is browned and filling is bubbly. (If pastry browns too quickly, cover loosely with foil.) Cool completely on a wire rack then remove sides of pan. Sprinkle top with sifted confectioners' sugar. Makes 16 servings.

PER SERVING		DAILY GOAL
Calories	455	2,000 (F), 2,500 (M)
Total Fat	26 g	60 g or less (F), 70 g or less (M)
Saturated fat	8 g	20 g or less (F), 23 g or less (M)
Cholesterol	58 mg	300 mg or less
Sodium	45 mg	2,400 mg or less
Carbohydrates	55 g	250 g or more
Protein	5 g	55 g to 90 g

93

PEACH MELBA TART

Peaches are baked over an almond-sugar layer and adorned with fresh raspberries. It's an elegant ending to any meal.

Ⓜ *Microwave*
Prep time: 30 minutes plus chilling
Baking time: 63 to 65 minutes
◗ *Degree of difficulty: moderate*

1   **9½-inch Ultimate Tart Pastry (recipe, page 9)**

Filling
½   **cup granulated sugar**
½   **cup blanched slivered almonds**
1   **tablespoon cornstarch**
1   **large egg**
2½ **pounds ripe peaches, peeled and quartered (5 cups)**
¼   **cup peach *or* apricot preserves**
1   **cup fresh raspberries**

1 Prepare Ultimate Tart Pastry as directed, except do not prick dough. Bake only 10 minutes, then remove foil and beans. Bake pastry 8 to 10 minutes more or until golden. Cool completely on wire rack.

2 For filling, process the sugar with the almonds and cornstarch in a food processor until finely ground. Add the egg and process just until blended. Spread in the bottom of the baked pastry shell. Arrange the peaches on top.

3 Place tart on a cookie sheet and bake for 45 minutes or until golden. Cool on a wire rack for 5 minutes, then remove side of pan. Microwave preserves in a microwave-proof glass measure on high (100% power) for 1 minute. Brush the preserves over tart and cool completely. Arrange the raspberries around edge. Makes 8 servings.

PER SERVING		DAILY GOAL
Calories	360	2,000 (F), 2,500 (M)
Total fat	17 g	60 g or less (F), 70 g or less (M)
Saturated fat	8 g	20 g or less (F), 23 g or less (M)
Cholesterol	58 mg	300 mg or less
Sodium	49 mg	2,400 mg or less
Carbohydrates	50 g	250 g or more
Protein	5 g	55 g to 90 g

NOTES

PEACH TART TATIN

This dessert demands peaches that are picked at their peak in August and September. The result is a delicious variation of the classic Apple Tart Tatin.

Prep time: 30 minutes plus standing and freezing
Baking time: 25 minutes
Degree of difficulty: moderate

Pastry
1 cup all-purpose flour
2 teaspoons granulated sugar
 Pinch salt
⅓ cup cold butter, cut up
 (no substitutions)
3 to 4 tablespoons ice water

Filling
3 tablespoons butter, softened
 (no substitutions)
5 tablespoons granulated sugar
2 pounds ripe peaches, peeled and quartered

1 For pastry, combine the flour, sugar, and salt in a medium bowl. Cut in the butter with a pastry blender or 2 knives until mixture resembles coarse crumbs. Add water, 1 tablespoon at a time, tossing with a fork until pastry just begins to hold together. Shape into a thick disk. Wrap in plastic wrap and refrigerate 1 hour or overnight.

2 On a lightly floured surface with a floured rolling pin, roll pastry ⅜-inch thick and cut into a 9-inch circle. Transfer circle to a cookie sheet lined with wax paper and freeze for 1 hour.

3 Preheat oven to 425°F. For filling, spread the butter over bottom and sides of a 10-inch cast iron skillet. Sprinkle bottom and sides with the sugar. Arrange the peaches, pitted side up, in 2 tight, concentric circles in skillet. Cook over medium-high heat, shaking and swirling skillet frequently, for 10 to 12 minutes or until sugar is caramelized and golden brown.

4 Place a cookie sheet on center oven rack. Invert frozen crust over fruit in skillet and remove wax paper. Place skillet on cookie sheet and bake about 25 minutes or until crust is well browned.

5 Remove skillet from oven. Let cool 15 minutes. Invert tart onto a serving dish with a rim. Serve warm or at room temperature. Makes 8 servings.

PER SERVING		DAILY GOAL
Calories	233	2,000 (F), 2,500 (M)
Total fat	12 g	60 g or less (F), 70 g or less (M)
Saturated fat	7 g	20 g or less (F), 23 g or less (M)
Cholesterol	32 mg	300 mg or less
Sodium	138 mg	2,400 mg or less
Carbohydrates	30 g	250 g or more
Protein	2 g	55 g to 90 g

NOTES

_____

_____

_____

_____

_____

_____

_____

_____

_____

PLUM FRANGIPANE TART

Fresh plums star in this nutty, autumnal tart, fragrant with orange and a touch of cloves.

Ⓜ *Microwave*
Prep time: 40 minutes plus chilling
Baking time: 45 to 55 minutes
◐ *Degree of difficulty: moderate*

1 **9½-inch Ultimate Tart Pastry (recipe, page 9)**

Filling

¾ **cup blanched almonds**
⅓ **cup confectioners' sugar**
1 **tablespoon all-purpose flour Pinch cloves**
1 **large egg**
1 **tablespoon butter, softened, cut up**
¼ **teaspoon grated orange peel (optional)**
1½ **pounds small ripe plums, quartered (about 6)**
2 **tablespoons granulated sugar**

2 **tablespoons apricot *or* peach preserves Water**

1 Prepare Ultimate Tart Pastry as directed through Steps 1 and 2, except do not prick dough. *(Do not follow steps 3 and 4.)*

2 Preheat oven to 375°F. For filling, combine the almonds, confectioners' sugar, flour, and cloves in a food processor and process until finely ground. Add the egg, butter, and orange peel and blend until incorporated. Spoon into prepared pastry shell. Arrange the plums on top and sprinkle with granulated sugar. Bake for 45 to 55 minutes or until plums are tender and filling is lightly browned.

3 Microwave preserves with 1 teaspoon water in a microwave-proof glass measure on high (100% power) for 30 seconds or until melted. Brush over warm tart. Remove sides of pan then cool completely on a wire rack. Makes 8 servings.

PER SERVING		DAILY GOAL
Calories	365	2,000 (F), 2,500 (M)
Total fat	21 g	60 g or less (F), 70 g or less (M)
Saturated fat	9 g	20 g or less (F), 23 g or less (M)
Cholesterol	61 mg	300 mg or less
Sodium	62 mg	2,400 mg or less
Carbohydrates	40 g	250 g or more
Protein	6 g	55 g to 90 g

NOTES

PLUM-GINGER TARTS

Fresh plums are available from May through September. Juicy and sweet, we like the dark red and purple skin varieties.

Ⓜ *Microwave*
   Prep time: 1 hour plus chilling and
      freezing
   Baking time: 20 to 25 minutes
◐ *Degree of difficulty: moderate*

   Ultimate Tart Pastry
      (recipe, page 9)
   Water
 4 **large ripe plums, halved and pitted**
   Granulated sugar
 ⅓ **cup apricot preserves**
 ½ **teaspoon grated fresh ginger**
   Confectioners' sugar
   Sweetened whipped cream
      (optional)

1 Prepare pastry for Ultimate Tart Pastry as directed through Step 1, except divide dough in half and shape into 2 disks. Wrap disks tightly and refrigerate 1 hour or overnight. *(Do not follow steps 2, 3, and 4.)*

2 On a lightly floured surface with a floured rolling pin, roll 1 pastry disk into an 11-inch square, then trim pastry to a 10-inch square. Cut into quarters to make four 5-inch squares. Transfer squares to a cookie sheet and repeat process with the remaining pastry disk. Chill 15 minutes.

3 Cut a ½-inch border inside each square, leaving 2 opposite corners uncut. Lightly brush water over the ½-inch area just inside the cut areas. Lift up 1 cut corner and fold it over to the opposite side, gently pressing it over the moistened pastry. Repeat process with opposite cut corner. (Strips will form a raised border and the uncut corners will twist decoratively.) Freeze for 30 minutes.

4 Preheat oven to 425°F. Arrange the plums cut side down on a work surface. Keeping halves together to maintain their shape, cut into ¼-inch-thick slices. Place 1 sliced plum half in center of each pastry square and press down gently to fan fruit. Sprinkle about 1 teaspoon granulated sugar over the top of each tart. Bake for 20 to 25 minutes or until fruit is bubbly and pastry is golden. Cool tarts on a wire rack.

5 Combine the apricot preserves and ginger in a microwave-proof 1-cup glass measure. Microwave on high (100% power) for 45 seconds or until melted. Strain preserves through a fine sieve into a small bowl. Brush preserves generously over tarts. Sprinkle with confectioners' sugar and serve with whipped cream, if desired. Makes 8 tarts.

PER SERVING WITHOUT WHIPPED CREAM		DAILY GOAL
Calories	250	2,000 (F), 2,500 (M)
Total fat	12 g	60 g or less (F), 70 g or less (M)
Saturated fat	7 g	20 g or less (F), 23 g or less (M)
Cholesterol	31 mg	300 mg or less
Sodium	42 mg	2,400 mg or less
Carbohydrates	34 g	250 g or more
Protein	2 g	55 g to 90 g

NOTES

_____

_____

_____

_____

_____

_____

FREE-FORM APPLE TARTS

Preparing these tarts from the premier dessert cookbook author Maida Heatter is a joy. The buttery pastry is quickly made in the food processor. And, both the pastry and filling can be made ahead.

Prep time: 1 hour plus chilling
Baking time: 30 to 35 minutes
◐ *Degree of difficulty: moderate*

Pastry
- 1 cup all-purpose flour
- 1 tablespoon granulated sugar
- ¼ teaspoon salt
- ½ cup cold butter, cut up
- 3 tablespoons ice water

Filling
- ¼ cup granulated sugar
- ¼ cup water
- 3 tablespoons butter
- 1 tablespoon grated lemon peel
- 1 teaspoon cinnamon
  Pinch nutmeg
- 2 pounds tart green apples, peeled, cored and cut into 1-inch pieces
- ¼ cup dark raisins
- ⅓ cup walnuts, coarsely chopped
- 1 large egg yolk
  Water
  Granulated sugar
- ⅓ cup apricot preserves

1 For pastry, combine the flour, sugar, and salt in a food processor with a steel blade. Add the butter and pulse 4 to 5 times. With machine on, add ice water all at once through feed tube and process for 7 or 8 seconds or just until mixture is crumbly.

2 On a lightly floured surface, gently press pastry together into an even log. Divide pastry into quarters, then shape into disks. Wrap and refrigerate 30 minutes or overnight.

3 For filling, combine sugar, water, butter, lemon peel, cinnamon, and nutmeg in a large skillet. Cook, stirring, over high heat until butter is melted. Stir in apples, cover and cook 5 minutes. Cook uncovered, stirring frequently, about 5 minutes more or until liquid is evaporated. Stir in raisins. Cool completely. Stir in the nuts.

4 Preheat oven to 450°F. On a lightly floured surface with a floured rolling pin, roll each pastry disk into a 7-inch circle. Transfer each to an ungreased cookie sheet, then refrigerate 15 minutes. Whisk yolk and 1 tablespoon water together in a cup.

5 Spoon a quarter of the filling in the center of each pastry circle, mounding it high and leaving a 1½-inch border. Brush border with water. Working quickly, raise each border, pinching deep pleats about 1 inch apart. Fold pleats over to rest against filling. Brush egg mixture on sides and sprinkle filling with sugar. Bake 5 minutes. Reduce oven temperature to 400°F. Bake 25 to 30 minutes more or until golden.

6 Meanwhile, melt the preserves in a saucepan over medium heat. Strain through a fine sieve. Return preserves to saucepan and keep warm. Transfer tarts to a wire rack. Immediately brush preserves over tops and sides of tarts. Serve warm or at room temperature. Makes 4 servings.

PER SERVING		DAILY GOAL	
Calories	740	2,000 (F), 2,500 (M)	
Total fat	40 g	60 g or less (F), 70 g or less (M)	
Saturated fat	20 g	20 g or less (F), 23 g or less (M)	
Cholesterol	139 mg	300 mg or less	
Sodium	472 mg	2,400 mg or less	
Carbohydrates	96 g	250 g or more	
Protein	6 g	55 g to 90 g	

FIG AND PEAR TART

An exceptionally rich and flaky sour cream pastry is baked free-form on a cookie sheet and topped with an unusual combination of fresh figs and pears.

Prep time: 30 minutes plus chilling
Baking time: 25 to 35 minutes
● *Degree of difficulty: moderate*

Pastry
- ½ **cup cold butter, cut up (no substitutions)**
- 1 **cup all-purpose flour**
- ¼ **cup sour cream**
- 4 **tablespoons granulated sugar, divided**

Filling
- 2 **Bosc pears, unpeeled and cut into 16 wedges each**
- 4 **fresh figs (5 to 6 ounces), quartered**
- 2 **tablespoons granulated sugar**
- ½ **cup mascarpone cheese**
- 1 **tablespoon honey**

1 For pastry, cut the butter into the flour with a pastry blender or 2 knives until mixture resembles coarse crumbs. Stir in the sour cream. Knead on a lightly floured surface just to form a ball, then flatten into a 5-inch square. Wrap and refrigerate 2 hours or overnight.

2 On a lightly floured surface with a floured rolling pin, roll pastry to a 12x8-inch rectangle. Sprinkle evenly with 2 tablespoons of the sugar, then fold pastry into thirds, letter-style. Wrap and refrigerate 30 minutes.

3 Place pastry on a lightly floured surface and with an open end facing you, roll to a 15-inch-long strip. Sprinkle evenly with the remaining 2 tablespoons sugar and fold up again, letter-style. Wrap and refrigerate for 30 minutes more.

4 Roll pastry to a 13-inch square. Transfer to a large, ungreased cookie sheet. With a sharp knife, trim to a 13-inch circle. Refrigerate or freeze for 10 minutes.

5 Preheat oven to 375°F. For filling, arrange the pears, overlapping, with rounded side at outer edge of pastry circle. Layer the figs in a smaller circle in the center. Sprinkle with sugar. Bake 25 to 35 minutes or until pastry is golden and fruit is tender. Slide a long, flexible metal spatula under pastry to loosen. Cool on pan on a wire rack.

6 To serve, combine the mascarpone and honey. Add a dollop to each serving. Makes 8 servings.

PER SERVING		DAILY GOAL
Calories	320	2,000 (F), 2,500 (M)
Total fat	20 g	60 g or less (F), 70 g or less (M)
Saturated fat	8 g	20 g or less (F), 23 g or less (M)
Cholesterol	54 mg	300 mg or less
Sodium	130 mg	2,400 mg or less
Carbohydrates	34 g	250 g or more
Protein	3 g	55 g to 90 g

NOTES

_____

_____

_____

_____

_____

_____

_____

_____

AL FORNO'S APRICOT TARTS

These rustic tarts are from the trendy restaurant Al Forno, in Providence, Rhode Island, owned by husband and wife team George Germon and Johanne Killeen.

Prep time: 30 minutes plus chilling
Baking time: 25 to 30 minutes
○ *Degree of difficulty: easy*

Single Flaky Pastry (recipe, page 7)
1 **box (11 ounces) dried apricots**
2 **tablespoons granulated sugar**
3½ **tablespoons superfine sugar**
2 **tablespoons unsalted butter, cut into 4 pieces (no substitutions)**
Confectioners' sugar

1 Prepare pastry for Single Flaky Pastry crust as directed through step 1, except divide pastry into 4 equal pieces. *(Do not follow steps 2 and 3.)*

2 On a lightly floured surface with a floured rolling pin, roll each piece into a 7-inch circle. Transfer circles to 2 ungreased cookie sheets. Turn edges under and flute.

Prick bottoms of pastry shells with a fork; refrigerate.

3 Meanwhile, for filling, soak the apricots in water to cover in a medium saucepan for 1 hour. Bring to a boil over high heat. Add the granulated sugar, then reduce heat and simmer gently about 10 minutes or until apricots are plump and soft but still whole. Drain apricots, reserving liquid; set apricots aside. Return the liquid to the saucepan and simmer until reduced to ¼ cup.

4 Preheat oven to 425°F. Arrange the apricots, skin side up, in concentric circles on pastry shells. Brush fruit with reserved cooking liquid. Sprinkle tarts with superfine sugar, then dot each tart with a piece of butter. Bake for 25 to 30 minutes or until crust is golden. Transfer to wire racks and cool. Sprinkle tarts lightly with confectioners' sugar, then cut each in half. Makes 8 servings.

PER SERVING		DAILY GOAL
Calories	345	2,000 (F), 2,500 (M)
Total fat	15 g	60 g or less (F), 70 g or less (M)
Saturated fat	8 g	20 g or less (F), 23 g or less (M)
Cholesterol	31 mg	300 mg or less
Sodium	160 mg	2,400 mg or less
Carbohydrates	51 g	250 g or more
Protein	4 g	55 g to 90 g

101

CRÈME BRÛLÈE TARTLETS

Hidden under the satiny custard sauce are raspberries and bananas. *Also pictured on page 86.*

Prep time: 1½ hours plus chilling
Baking time: 21 to 24 minutes
● *Degree of difficulty: moderate*

Pastry

1½ **cups all-purpose flour**
1½ **teaspoons granulated sugar**
½ **teaspoon salt**
½ **cup cold unsalted butter, cut-up**
6 **to 8 tablespoons ice water**

Custard Filling

2 **cups heavy *or* whipping cream**
6 **large egg yolks**
⅓ **cup granulated sugar**
 Pinch salt
½ **vanilla bean, split**
1 **cup fresh raspberries**
1 **ripe banana, thinly sliced**
12 **teaspoons brown sugar**

1 For pastry, combine the flour, sugar, and salt in a large bowl. Gradually add butter, tossing gently until all pieces are coated with flour. Cut in the butter until mixture resembles coarse crumbs. Sprinkle with ice water, 1 tablespoon at a time, tossing with a fork until pastry just begins to hold together. Shape pastry into a ball, kneading if necessary. Divide pastry into 2 balls. Flatten into thick disks. Wrap in plastic wrap and chill 1 hour or overnight.

2 For Custard Filling, scald the cream in a saucepan. Beat the yolks, sugar, and salt in a mixing bowl until pale and thick and mixture forms a ribbon when beaters are lifted. Gradually add scalded cream in a thin, steady stream until combined. Return mixture to saucepan and add vanilla bean. Cook, stirring constantly, over low heat for 20 to 25 minutes or until mixture is thick enough to coat the back of a spoon. Strain custard through a fine sieve into a clean bowl. Scrape seeds from vanilla bean with a small knife and add to custard, discarding bean. Cool to room temperature.

3 Meanwhile, roll a pastry disk between 2 sheets of lightly floured wax paper to a circle ⅛-inch thick. Remove top sheet and carefully drape pastry over three 4½-inch tartlet pans with removable bottoms.

Remove second piece of paper and gently press pastry into pans. Press rolling pin across top of pastry to trim excess. Cut ½-inch-wide strips from excess pastry and press along side of pastry. Prick pastry. Repeat process with remaining pastry circle and 3 more tartlet pans. Freeze pastry 15 minutes. Preheat oven to 425°F. Line each pan with foil and fill with dried beans. Place shells on a cookie sheet and bake for 10 minutes. Remove foil and beans; bake 10 to 13 minutes more or until golden. Cool. Remove sides from pans.

4 Arrange the raspberries and banana slices in pastry shells. Spoon custard evenly over top of fruit. Refrigerate until custard is set, at least 20 minutes or up to 2 hours. Preheat broiler. Arrange tartlets on a cookie sheet. Sift 2 teaspoons of brown sugar over each tartlet. Broil 4 inches from heat about 1 minute or until sugar is melted and caramelized. Refrigerate tartlets 30 minutes or up to 3 hours. Makes 6 servings.

PER SERVING		DAILY GOAL
Calories	690	2,000 (F), 2,500 (M)
Total fat	50 g	60 g or less (F), 70 g or less (M)
Saturated fat	29 g	20 g or less (F), 23 g or less (M)
Cholesterol	363 mg	300 mg or less
Sodium	248 mg	2,400 mg or less
Carbohydrates	54 g	250 g or more
Protein	8 g	55 g to 90 g

CHERRY-MASCARPONE TART

This tart takes full advantage of rich and creamy mascarpone cheese and seasonal fresh sweet cherries. In autumn, we love this tart with fresh figs, too.

Prep time: 30 minutes
Baking time: 26 to 30 minutes
○ *Degree of difficulty: easy*

Ultimate Tart Pastry (recipe, page 9)
1 **cup mascarpone cheese (*or* 6 ounces softened cream cheese mixed with ⅓ cup sour cream)**
2 **tablespoons confectioners' sugar**
¼ **teaspoon grated lemon peel**
1½ **pounds fresh sweet cherries, pitted *or* 1½ dozen fresh green *or* purple figs, stemmed and halved**

1 Prepare the Ultimate Tart Pastry as directed.

2 Stir the mascarpone cheese, sugar, and lemon peel in a small bowl until blended. Spread cheese mixture evenly in the bottom of the baked pastry shell. Arrange the cherries, cut side down, on top. Cover and refrigerate for up to 3 hours. Makes 8 servings.

PER SERVING		DAILY GOAL
Calories	365	2,000 (F), 2,500 (M)
Total fat	25 g	60 g or less (F), 70 g or less (M)
Saturated fat	7 g	20 g or less (F), 23 g or less (M)
Cholesterol	70 mg	300 mg or less
Sodium	53 mg	2,400 mg or less
Carbohydrates	31 g	250 g or more
Protein	4 g	55 g to 90 g

TART AND SOUL

Be creative! Brush the Ultimate Tart Pastry (recipe, page 9) with melted chocolate or melted preserves, or pipe in some sweetened whipped cream. Then, fill with the following selection of fresh fruits. (The quantity listed fills a 10-inch tart.)

• 3 cups raspberries, blueberries, blackberries, halved strawberries and/or any combination

• 4 large ripe fresh peaches, peeled and thinly sliced, thinly sliced nectarines and/or a combination

• 6 fresh plums or large apricots, thinly sliced

• 1½ dozen fresh green or purple figs, stemmed and halved

• 4 ripe pears, cored and thinly sliced

• 4 ripe bananas, thinly sliced

FRESH STRAWBERRY TART

Aqua, in San Francisco, is renowned for chef George Morrone's innovative ways with seafood. But regulars know they should also leave room for dessert, such as this delicate tart of fresh strawberries in a classic vanilla pastry cream.

Prep time: 40 minutes plus chilling
Cooking time: 18 to 20 minutes
Degree of difficulty: moderate

Sweet Pastry
1½ cups all-purpose flour
½ cup granulated sugar
    Pinch salt
10 tablespoons cold butter, cut up
    (no substitutions)
1 large egg

Pastry Cream
2 cups milk
6 tablespoons granulated sugar, divided
½ vanilla bean, split lengthwise
4 large egg yolks
2 tablespoons cornstarch

1 tablespoon butter
    (no substitutions)
2 pints fresh strawberries, hulled and halved

1 Preheat oven to 375°F. For Sweet Pastry, combine the flour, sugar, and salt in a food processor and pulse to combine. Add the butter and process until crumbly. Add the egg and process just until pastry holds together. Press dough evenly into a 12-inch tart pan with a removable bottom. Freeze for 15 minutes.

2 Line frozen pastry shell with foil and fill with dried beans or uncooked rice. Bake for 10 minutes. Remove foil and beans. Bake pastry for 8 to 10 minutes more or until golden. Cool completely on a wire rack.

3 For Pastry Cream, heat the milk, 3 tablespoons of the sugar, and the vanilla bean to boiling in a small saucepan. Meanwhile, whisk the egg yolks with the remaining 3 tablespoons sugar in a medium bowl, then whisk in the cornstarch. Gradually whisk the hot milk mixture into the yolks. Return mixture to saucepan and bring to a boil, whisking. Reduce heat and boil, stirring constantly, 1 minute. Remove

from heat and stir in the butter. Strain the pastry cream through a fine sieve into a small bowl. Cover surface with plastic wrap and chill.

4 To assemble, spread Pastry Cream evenly in bottom of baked crust. Arrange strawberry halves on top. Makes 10 servings.

PER SERVING		DAILY GOAL
Calories	335	2,000 (F), 2,500 (M)
Total fat	17 g	60 g or less (F), 70 g or less (M)
Saturated fat	10 g	20 g or less (F), 23 g or less (M)
Cholesterol	147 mg	300 mg or less
Sodium	177 mg	2,400 mg or less
Carbohydrates	40 g	250 g or more
Protein	6 g	55 g to 90 g

NOTES

_____

_____

_____

_____

_____

_____

_____

LEMON TART

Of this simple citrus dessert, caterer Nancy Kirby Harris says, "It's really nothing more than lemon bar cookies that look more sophisticated in a tart shell." You can substitute lime for the lemon and serve it plain or with a simple raspberry sauce.

> *Prep time: 10 to 15 minutes plus*
>   *cooling*
> *Baking time: 30 to 36 minutes*
> O *Degree of difficulty: easy*

Crust
- 1 **cup all-purpose flour**
- 7 **tablespoons butter, softened (no substitutions)**
- 2 **tablespoons confectioners' sugar**

Filling
- 3 **large eggs, lightly beaten**
- 1 **cup granulated sugar**
- ⅓ **cup fresh lemon juice**
- 2 **tablespoons all-purpose flour**
   Confectioners' sugar

1 Preheat oven to 350°F. For crust, combine the flour, butter, and confectioners' sugar in a food processor and process until combined. Press evenly into a 9-inch tart pan with a removable bottom or a springform pan. Refrigerate 15 minutes. Bake for 15 to 18 minutes or until a deep, golden brown. Leave oven on. Cool completely on a wire rack.

2 For filling, whisk the eggs, granulated sugar, lemon juice, and flour together in a large bowl until smooth. Pour into baked pastry shell. Bake for 15 to 18 minutes, or until filling is set. Transfer to a wire rack. Sift additional confectioners' sugar over the warm tart. Cool completely. Makes 8 servings.

PER SERVING		DAILY GOAL
Calories	290	2,000 (F), 2,500 (M)
Total fat	12 g	60 g or less (F), 70 g or less (M)
Saturated fat	7 g	20 g or less (F), 23 g or less (M)
Cholesterol	107 mg	300 mg or less
Sodium	127 mg	2,400 mg or less
Carbohydrates	42 g	250 g or more
Protein	4 g	55 g to 90 g

NOTES

RITZ-CARLTON'S FRESH FRUIT TART

A most-requested recipe from our readers, this lovely tart with a creamy amaretto filling can be topped with your choice of berries or sliced fresh fruit.

Ⓜ *Microwave*
Prep time: 45 minutes plus chilling
Baking time: 26 to 30 minutes
⬤ *Degree of difficulty: moderate*

1　**10-inch Ultimate Tart Pastry (recipe, page 9)**

Almond Pastry Cream
2　**cups milk**
3　**large egg yolks**
½　**cup granulated sugar**
⅓　**cup plus 1 tablespoon cornstarch**
2　**tablespoons butter** *or* **margarine**
2　**tablespoons amaretto liqueur**
¼　**teaspoon almond extract**
1　**cup heavy** *or* **whipping cream**
⅓　**cup apricot preserves**
1　**pint fresh strawberries, sliced**
2　**kiwi fruit, peeled and sliced**

1　Prepare Ultimate Tart Pastry as directed.

2　For Almond Pastry Cream, bring milk to a boil in a medium saucepan over medium-high heat. Meanwhile, whisk the yolks and sugar together in a small bowl, then whisk in the cornstarch. Gradually whisk the hot milk into the egg yolk mixture. Return to pan and bring to a boil, stirring constantly. Reduce heat and cook, stirring, 2 minutes more. Strain through a fine sieve into a medium bowl. Whisk in the butter, liqueur, and almond extract. Cover surface of cream with wax paper and cool, then refrigerate about 2 hours or until cold.

3　Whisk chilled Almond Pastry Cream just until smooth. Beat the heavy cream to stiff peaks in a small mixing bowl. Fold into pastry cream with a rubber spatula.

4　Place the apricot preserves in a 1-cup microwave-proof glass measure. Microwave on high (100% power) for 45 seconds or until melted. Strain preserves through a fine sieve into a small bowl and keep warm. Spread pastry cream in the baked pastry shell. Arrange fruit slices decoratively on top in concentric circles, then brush with apricot glaze. Serves 10.

PER SERVING		DAILY GOAL
Calories	400	2,000 (F), 2,500 (M)
Total fat	24 g	60 g or less (F), 70 g or less (M)
Saturated fat	14 g	20 g or less (F), 23 g or less (M)
Cholesterol	134 mg	300 mg or less
Sodium	93 mg	2,400 mg or less
Carbohydrates	42 g	250 g or more
Protein	5 g	55 g to 90 g

NOTES

_____
_____
_____
_____
_____
_____
_____
_____
_____
_____
_____

SAVORY MAIN-DISH

PIES AND TARTS

Who says pies have to be sweet? Here's a sampling of some of the best savory fillings ever put inside a buttery crust. Try creamy Leek and Mustard Tart or Spinach and Goat Cheese Tart. Or, make a meal of Sorrel-Onion Tart, Fresh Tomato Tart, or Three-Cheese Potato Pie. Just add a salad to any one of these flavorful gems and you've got a meal.

QUICHE LORRAINE

No collection of savory pies and tarts would be complete without this classic cheese and bacon entrée from France.

Prep time: 40 minutes plus chilling
Baking time: 30 to 35 minutes
O *Degree of difficulty: easy*

Single Flaky Pastry (recipe, page 7)
6 **slices bacon, cooked and crumbled**
1 **cup shredded Swiss cheese**
3 **large eggs**
2 **cups milk**
1 **tablespoon all-purpose flour**
½ **teaspoon salt**
⅛ **teaspoon nutmeg**
1 **tablespoon butter *or* margarine**

1 Prepare Single Flaky Pastry as directed.

2 Preheat oven to 425°F. Line pastry shell with foil and fill with dried beans or uncooked rice. Bake 12 minutes. Remove foil and beans. Bake pastry 5 minutes more. Cool completely on a wire rack.

3 Reduce oven temperature to 375°F. Sprinkle the bacon and cheese evenly on bottom of baked pie crust. Whisk the eggs with the milk, flour, salt, and nutmeg in a large bowl until combined, then pour over cheese. Melt butter in a small saucepan until lightly browned and drizzle over top.

4 Bake 30 to 35 minutes or until a knife inserted near center of quiche comes out clean. Cool on a wire rack for 15 minutes. Serve warm or at room temperature. Makes 8 servings.

PER SERVING		DAILY GOAL
Calories	360	2,000 (F), 2,500 (M)
Total fat	27 g	60 g or less (F), 70 g or less (M)
Saturated fat	13 g	20 g or less (F), 23 g or less (M)
Cholesterol	139 mg	300 mg or less
Sodium	502 mg	2,400 mg or less
Carbohydrates	19 g	250 g or more
Protein	12 g	55 g to 90 g

THREE-CHEESE POTATO PIE

Nothing could be easier! This crustless pie makes a splendid light supper for six—just add a tossed green salad and crusty bread.

Prep time: 20 minutes
Baking time: 60 to 70 minutes
O *Degree of difficulty: easy*

2 **large eggs, lightly beaten**
2 **cups mashed potatoes**
1 **cup finely chopped onions**
1 **cup shredded Swiss cheese**
1 **cup sour cream**
½ **cup cottage cheese**
⅓ **cup chopped green onions**
¼ **cup freshly grated Parmesan cheese**
½ **teaspoon salt**
¼ **teaspoon freshly ground pepper**

1 Preheat oven to 350°F. Grease a 10-inch deep-dish pie plate.

2 Combine the eggs, mashed potatoes, chopped onions, Swiss cheese, sour cream, cottage cheese, green onions, Parmesan cheese, salt, and pepper in a large bowl until well blended. Pour into the prepared pie plate. Bake for 60 to 70 minutes or until filling is puffed and evenly browned on top. Makes 6 servings.

PER SERVING		DAILY GOAL
Calories	300	2,000 (F), 2,500 (M)
Total fat	20 g	60 g or less (F), 70 g or less (M)
Saturated fat	10 g	20 g or less (F), 23 g or less (M)
Cholesterol	112 mg	300 mg or less
Sodium	627 mg	2,400 mg or less
Carbohydrates	17 g	250 g or more
Protein	14 g	55 g to 90 g

SAY CHEESE

Cheddar: Whether you use yellow or white cheddar, domestic or imported, we recommend sharp or extra-sharp for maximum flavor.

Cantal: A member of the cheddar family, this firm cheese from France has a rich golden color and a nutty-sweet flavor.

Cheshire: A rich cow's milk cheese imported from England. It has a semi-firm, creamy texture with a mild, tangy flavor. A medium-sharp cheddar can be substituted.

Feta: Available in 8 ounce blocks or crumbled. This flavorful cheese is creamy, sharp, and assertive, and a little goes a long way. It's great used in combination with other milder cheeses.

Goat Cheese: Available in small and large logs, fresh goat cheese is perfect for crumbling and melting and its tangy flavor is perfect with fresh herbs and vegetables.

Mascarpone: There's really no substitute for this ultra-rich cheese with just a hint of sweetness. Perfectly paired with fruit.

Mozzarella: This mild, delicately flavored cheese has superior melting quality. Choose from fresh, whole milk, or part-skim.

Parmesan: For this deeply rich and nutty cheese, quality makes a difference—in both depth of flavor and meltability; Parmigiano Reggiano is the finest. Most important is to purchase this cheese in blocks and freshly grate it just before serving.

Ricotta: A moist, mildly sweet cheese. Choose from whole milk or part-skim varieties.

Swiss Cheese: Pale yellow, meltable, and slightly nutty. Emmentaler and Gruyère cheeses from Switzerland are the most famous. Imported Jarlsberg and many domestic varieties are other good choices.

GREEK-STYLE GREENS PIE

Here's a wonderful meatless entrée that's perfect for lunch or as a light supper. Serve warm or at room temperature.

Prep time: 50 to 60 minutes
Baking time: 1 hour
Degree of difficulty: easy

½ cup water
1 pound fresh spinach, stems removed, coarsely chopped
½ pound escarole, coarsely chopped
½ pound chicory, coarsely chopped
2 tablespoons butter *or* margarine
1 cup chopped onions
¼ cup chopped fresh parsley
3 tablespoons chopped fresh dill
½ teaspoon freshly ground pepper
¼ teaspoon salt
 Pinch nutmeg
4 ounces goat cheese, crumbled
4 ounces feta cheese, crumbled
1 large egg, lightly beaten
⅓ cup butter *or* margarine, melted
16 sheets (about ½ pound) phyllo dough

1 For filling, bring water to a boil in a large Dutch oven. Add the spinach, escarole, and chicory. Cover and cook, stirring occasionally, about 5 minutes or until greens are wilted. Drain greens in a colander, pressing out excess liquid.

2 Melt the butter in a large skillet over medium-high heat. Add the onions and cook about 3 minutes or until tender. Add cooked greens, parsley, dill, pepper, salt, and nutmeg and cook 2 minutes more. Cool greens mixture then add the goat cheese, feta cheese, and egg, mixing well.

3 Preheat oven to 425°F. Brush a 9-inch metal pie pan with melted butter. Place 1 phyllo sheet in pie pan, letting sides overhang. Brush lightly with butter to 1 inch beyond edge of plate. Layer and butter 7 more sheets. Spoon in greens filling. Layer and butter remaining phyllo on top, then trim edges of phyllo with scissors to form a 1-inch overhang. Tuck overhang under and flute edge. Bake for 30 minutes. Reduce oven temperature to 375°F. Bake for 30 minutes more or until golden. Makes 8 servings.

PER SERVING		DAILY GOAL
Calories	250	2,000 (F), 2,500 (M)
Total fat	20 g	60 g or less (F), 70 g or less (M)
Saturated fat	12 g	20 g or less (F), 23 g or less (M)
Cholesterol	78 mg	300 mg or less
Sodium	616 mg	2,400 mg or less
Carbohydrates	22 g	250 g or more
Protein	11 g	55 g to 90 g

NOTES

SCALLION PIE

This Southern-style homey pie with an old-fashioned lard pastry is from chef, teacher, and cookbook author Edna Lewis.

Prep time: 30 minutes plus chilling
Baking time: 60 to 70 minutes
Degree of difficulty: moderate

Pastry

2½	**cups unbleached all-purpose flour**
1	**teaspoon salt**
10	**tablespoons chilled lard *or* vegetable shortening**
4 to 5	**tablespoons ice water**

Filling

⅓	**cup water**
6	**cups sliced green onions**
⅔	**cup heavy *or* whipping cream**
½	**teaspoon minced garlic**
½	**teaspoon salt**
¼	**teaspoon freshly ground pepper**

1 For pastry, combine the flour and salt in a large bowl. Add the lard, tossing gently until all pieces are coated with flour. With a pastry blender or 2 knives, cut in lard until mixture resembles coarse crumbs. Sprinkle with ice water, 1 tablespoon at a time, tossing vigorously with a fork until pastry just begins to hold together. On a smooth surface, shape pastry into a ball, kneading lightly if necessary. Divide pastry into 2 balls, 1 slightly larger than the other. Flatten into 2 thick disks. Wrap tightly in plastic wrap and refrigerate 30 minutes.

2 For filling, bring the water to a boil in a large skillet over high heat. Add the green onions and cook, stirring, for 2 minutes or until green tops are wilted; drain. Add the cream, garlic, salt, and pepper to skillet. Bring to a boil and cook about 4 minutes or until reduced to ½ cup. Set aside.

3 Preheat oven to 350°F. On a lightly floured surface with a floured rolling pin, roll larger disk into a 12-inch circle and fit into a 9-inch pie pan, leaving a 1-inch overhang. Spoon filling into pastry shell. Brush overhang with water. Roll remaining pastry into an 11-inch circle. Cut vents and place on top of filling. Trim and flute edge of pastry. Bake 60 to 70 minutes or until pastry is golden brown. Serve warm. Makes 8 servings.

PER SERVING		DAILY GOAL
Calories	390	2,000 (F), 2,500 (M)
Total fat	24 g	60 g or less (F), 70 g or less (M)
Saturated fat	11 g	20 g or less (F), 23 g or less (M)
Cholesterol	42 mg	300 mg or less
Sodium	436 mg	2,400 mg or less
Carbohydrates	38 g	250 g or more
Protein	6 g	55 g to 90 g

NOTES

CURRY PIE

Here's a twist on the classic Shepherd's Pie. Our version has a buttery sweet potato topping.

Prep time: 50 minutes
Baking time: 25 to 30 minutes
○ *Degree of difficulty: easy*

Topping
- 2 **pounds sweet potatoes**
- 2 **tablespoons butter** *or* **margarine**
- ¾ **teaspoon salt**
- ½ **teaspoon freshly ground pepper**

Filling
- 1 **tablespoon vegetable oil**
- 1 **cup chopped onions**
- 1 **tablespoon minced jalapeño chiles**
- 2 **teaspoons minced garlic**
- 1 **tablespoon curry powder**
- 2 **teaspoons cumin**
- 2 **teaspoons coriander**
- 2 **teaspoons turmeric**
- ¾ **teaspoon salt**
- ¾ **teaspoon freshly ground pepper**
- ½ **teaspoon cinnamon**
- ¼ **teaspoon allspice**
- ¾ **pound ground beef**
- ¾ **pound ground pork**
- 1 **can (14½ ounces) tomatoes, undrained and chopped**
- 2 **cups small cauliflower florets**
- 1 **cup frozen peas**

1 For topping, combine the sweet potatoes with salted water to cover in a large saucepan. Bring to a boil, then cover and cook about 30 minutes or until fork-tender. Drain and peel. Mash potatoes in a large bowl. Add the butter, salt, and pepper and beat until smooth.

2 Meanwhile, for filling, heat the oil in a large skillet over medium-high heat. Add the onions, chiles, and garlic and cook about 2 minutes or until tender. Add the curry, cumin, coriander, turmeric, salt, pepper, cinnamon, and allspice and cook 1 minute. Stir in the ground beef and ground pork and cook about 5 minutes or until meat is browned. Stir in the tomatoes with their liquid and the cauliflower. Reduce heat; cover and simmer for 10 minutes. Stir in the peas.

3 Preheat oven to 375°F. Transfer filling to a shallow 2-quart glass baking dish. Spoon topping into a pastry bag fitted with a large star tip and pipe decoratively on filling. (Or, spread topping over filling with a rubber spatula.) Bake pie for 25 to 30 minutes or until bubbly. Makes 6 to 8 servings.

PER SERVING		DAILY GOAL	
Calories	475	2,000 (F), 2,500 (M)	
Total fat	29 g	60 g or less (F), 70 g or less (M)	
Saturated fat	11 g	20 g or less (F), 23 g or less (M)	
Cholesterol	85 mg	300 mg or less	
Sodium	702 mg	2,400 mg or less	
Carbohydrates	33 g	250 g or more	
Protein	21 g	55 g to 90 g	

NOTES

_____

_____

_____

_____

_____

_____

_____

_____

_____

CHICKEN AND SPINACH PIE

Don't be daunted by the long list of ingredients for this unusual pie from cookbook author Beatrice Ojakangas. The taste of this dish makes every one of them count.

Prep time: 50 minutes plus chilling
Baking time: 45 to 50 minutes
Degree of difficulty: moderate

Cornmeal Pastry
1⅔ cups all-purpose flour
¼ cup yellow cornmeal
1 teaspoon salt
¾ cup cold unsalted butter, cut up (no substitutions)
1 large egg, lightly beaten
2 teaspoons white vinegar
1 to 2 tablespoons ice water

Chicken Filling
1¼ pounds boneless, skinless chicken breasts
1½ teaspoons salt, divided
2 packages (10 ounces each) frozen chopped spinach, thawed

1 tablespoon olive oil
1 tablespoon butter *or* margarine
1½ teaspoons minced garlic
¼ cup raisins
¼ cup pine nuts *or* slivered almonds, toasted
4 ounces thinly sliced prosciutto *or* other ham, julienned
2 large eggs, lightly beaten
¾ cup heavy cream *or* evaporated milk

1 For Cornmeal Pastry, combine the flour, cornmeal, and salt in a medium bowl. With a pastry blender or 2 knives, cut in the butter until mixture resembles coarse crumbs. In a small bowl, combine the egg, vinegar, and 1 tablespoon ice water. Sprinkle over cornmeal mixture, stirring with a fork, just until dough holds together, adding more water if necessary. On a smooth surface, shape pastry into a ball, kneading lightly if necessary. Divide pastry into 2 pieces, 1 slightly larger than the other. Flatten into 2 thick disks. Wrap tightly in plastic wrap; chill 30 minutes or overnight.

2 Meanwhile, for Chicken Filling, combine the chicken with 1 teaspoon of the salt and water to cover in a large saucepan; bring to a boil. Reduce heat and

simmer gently 10 minutes. Drain, then cool to room temperature. Shred into bite-size pieces.

3 Squeeze excess liquid from frozen spinach. Heat oil and butter in a large skillet over medium-high heat. Add spinach, garlic, raisins, pine nuts, and prosciutto. Cook, stirring occasionally, for 5 minutes or until liquid is evaporated. Transfer to a large bowl. Add chicken, eggs, cream, remaining ½ teaspoon salt, and ¼ teaspoon freshly ground pepper.

4 Preheat oven to 350°F. Between 2 sheets of floured wax paper, roll larger disk into an 11-inch circle and fit into a 9-inch pie pan, leaving a 1-inch overhang. Spoon filling into pie pan and brush overhang with water. Roll remaining pastry into a 10-inch circle. Cut vents and place on top of filling. Trim and flute edge of pastry. Bake for 45 to 50 minutes or until pastry is golden brown. Serve warm. Makes 8 servings.

PER SERVING		DAILY GOAL
Calories	550	2,000 (F), 2,500 (M)
Total fat	35 g	60 g or less (F), 70 g or less (M)
Saturated fat	19 g	20 g or less (F), 23 g or less (M)
Cholesterol	210 mg	300 mg or less
Sodium	910 mg	2,400 mg or less
Carbohydrates	31 g	250 g or more
Protein	29 g	55 g to 90 g

LEEK AND MUSTARD TART

Here's a fabulous main-dish tart from the celebrated vegetarian restaurant Greens, in San Francisco. The sharp cheddar cheese and Dijon mustard give a little bite to the natural sweetness of the leeks.

Prep time: 45 minutes plus chilling
Baking time: 55 minutes
● *Degree of difficulty: moderate*

Savory Tart Pastry (recipe, page 9)
3 **tablespoons butter (no substitutions)**
4 **to 5 cups sliced leeks (about 1 pound, trimmed)**
½ **cup dry white wine** *or* **water**
½ **teaspoon salt**
¼ **teaspoon freshly ground pepper**
2 **large eggs**
1 **cup heavy** *or* **whipping cream** *or* **crème fraîche**
1 **to 2 tablespoons smooth** *or* **coarse Dijon mustard**
¾ **cup shredded cheddar** *or* **Cantal cheese**
2 **tablespoons snipped chives**

1 Prepare Savory Tart Pastry as directed.

2 On a lightly floured surface with a floured rolling pin, roll pastry into an ⅛-inch-thick circle and fit into a 9½-inch tart pan with a removable bottom or a 9-inch pie plate. Gently press pastry with fingertips along bottom and up side of pan. With scissors, trim pastry to 1 inch above edge. Fold overhanging pastry into side of crust and gently press edge up to extend ¼ inch above side of pan. Freeze pastry shell for 15 minutes.

3 Preheat oven to 425°F. Line frozen pastry shell with foil and fill with dried beans or uncooked rice. Bake for 10 minutes. Remove foil and beans. Bake pastry 5 minutes more or until pale golden. Cool completely on wire rack. Leave oven on and adjust oven rack to lowest position.

4 Melt the butter in a large skillet over medium heat. Add the leeks and cook for 2 to 3 minutes or until softened. Carefully add the wine, salt, and pepper. Reduce heat to low; cover and cook for 10 to 15 minutes or until leeks are very tender. If necessary, add more wine after 7 minutes.

5 Beat the eggs with the cream and mustard in a large bowl. Stir in the leeks and shredded cheese. Pour filling into baked tart shell. Smooth top and sprinkle on chives. Place the filled pastry shell on the lowest oven rack. Bake for 10 minutes. Reduce oven temperature to 375°F. Bake for 30 minutes more or until filling is set and golden. Let stand for 5 minutes before serving. Makes 6 servings.

PER SERVING		DAILY GOAL
Calories	540	2,000 (F), 2,500 (M)
Total fat	39 g	60 g or less (F), 70 g or less (M)
Saturated fat	22 g	20 g or less (F), 23 g or less (M)
Cholesterol	176 mg	300 mg or less
Sodium	754 mg	2,400 mg or less
Carbohydrates	37 g	250 g or more
Protein	11 g	55 g to 90 g

NOTES

_____

_____

_____

_____

_____

SPINACH AND GOAT CHEESE TART

In this savory tart from Greens, a vegetarian restaurant in San Francisco, use a creamy goat cheese such as a Bucheron or Lezay, or feta. If you do use feta cheese, reduce the amount of salt in the recipe.

Prep time: 45 minutes plus chilling
Baking time: 55 minutes
Degree of difficulty: moderate

Savory Tart Pastry (recipe, page 9)
3 **tablespoons butter (no substitutions)**
2 **bunches green onions, white part only, thinly sliced**
1½ **teaspoons minced garlic**
1 **tablespoon fresh marjoram leaves or ½ teaspoon dried**
1 **tablespoon chopped fresh parsley**
1 **bag (10 ounces) fresh spinach, rinsed well**
¾ **teaspoon salt, divided**
½ **teaspoon freshly ground pepper, divided**
2 **large eggs**
1 **large egg yolk**
4 **ounces goat cheese, crumbled and divided**
¾ **to 1 cup milk**
¾ **to 1 cup heavy *or* whipping cream Pinch nutmeg**

1 Prepare Savory Tart Pastry as directed.

2 On a lightly floured surface with a floured rolling pin, roll pastry into an ⅛-inch-thick circle and fit into a 9½-inch tart pan with a removable bottom or a 9-inch pie plate. Gently press pastry with fingertips along bottom and up side of pan. With scissors, trim pastry to 1 inch above edge. Fold overhanging pastry into side of crust and gently press edge up to extend ¼ inch above side of pan. Freeze pastry shell for 15 minutes.

3 Preheat oven to 425°F. Line frozen pastry shell with foil and fill with dried beans or uncooked rice. Bake for 10 minutes. Remove foil and beans. Bake pastry for 5 minutes more or until pale golden. Cool completely on wire rack. Leave oven on and adjust oven rack to lowest position.

4 Melt the butter in a large skillet over medium heat. Add the green onions, garlic, marjoram, and parsley and cook for 1 minute. Gradually add the spinach in batches, letting each batch begin to soften and wilt before adding the next. Season with ¼ teaspoon of the salt and ¼ teaspoon of the pepper. Drain spinach mixture in a colander, squeezing out any excess moisture.

5 Beat the eggs with the egg yolk and 2 ounces of the cheese in a large bowl. Add the milk, cream, nutmeg, the remaining ½ teaspoon salt, and the remaining ¼ teaspoon pepper. Spread spinach mixture on bottom of baked tart shell. Crumble the remaining 2 ounces of cheese on top and pour custard over all. Place the filled pastry shell on the lowest oven rack. Bake for 10 minutes. Reduce oven temperature to 375°F. and bake 30 minutes more or until filling is set and golden. Let stand 5 minutes before serving. Makes 6 servings.

PER SERVING		DAILY GOAL	
Calories	540	2,000 (F), 2,500 (M)	
Total fat	40 g	60 g or less (F), 70 g or less (M)	
Saturated fat	22 g	20 g or less (F), 23 g or less (M)	
Cholesterol	210 mg	300 mg or less	
Sodium	788 mg	2,400 mg or less	
Carbohydrates	32 g	250 g or more	
Protein	14 g	55 g to 90 g	

SORREL-ONION TART

This tart is based on a recipe from Richard Olney's "Simple French Food." The almost lemony, tart taste of fresh sorrel is very pleasing with the sweet, stewed onions.

Prep time: 30 to 35 minutes plus chilling
Baking time: 50 to 55 minutes
Degree of difficulty: moderate

Savory Tart Pastry (recipe, page 9)
4 **tablespoons butter, divided (no substitutions)**
1 **large red onion, thinly sliced**
½ **teaspoon salt**
4 **ounces fresh sorrel leaves (8 cups loosely packed), trimmed and sliced**
2 **large eggs**
1 **cup heavy or whipping cream**
¼ **teaspoon freshly ground pepper**
½ **cup shredded mozzarella cheese, divided**

1 Prepare Savory Tart Pastry as directed.

2 On a lightly floured surface with a floured rolling pin, roll pastry into an ⅛-inch-thick circle and fit into a 9½-inch tart pan with a removable bottom or a 9-inch pie plate. Gently press pastry with fingertips along bottom and up side of pan. With scissors, trim pastry to 1 inch above edge. Fold overhanging pastry into side of crust and gently press edge up to extend ¼ inch above side of pan. Freeze pastry shell for 15 minutes.

3 Preheat oven to 425°F. Line frozen pastry shell with foil and fill with dried beans or uncooked rice. Bake for 10 minutes. Remove foil and beans. Bake pastry for 5 minutes more or until pale golden. Cool completely on wire rack. Reduce oven temperature to 375°F. and adjust oven rack to lowest position.

4 Melt 3 tablespoons of the butter in a small skillet over medium heat. Add the onion and salt then cover and cook, stirring occasionally, about 10 minutes or until onion is tender.

5 Meanwhile, melt the remaining 1 tablespoon butter in a large skillet over low heat. Stir in the sorrel, a large handful at a time, and cook until wilted, 3 to 4 minutes.

6 Place baked pastry shell in pan on a cookie sheet. Whisk together the eggs, cream, and pepper in a large bowl, then stir in the onion, sorrel, and ¼ cup of the mozzarella. Sprinkle the remaining ¼ cup cheese over pastry, then pour filling on top. Place the filled pastry shell on the lowest oven rack. Bake for 35 to 40 minutes or until filling is set and golden. Makes 6 servings.

PER SERVING		DAILY GOAL
Calories	495	2,000 (F), 2,500 (M)
Total fat	38 g	60 g or less (F), 70 g or less (M)
Saturated fat	21 g	20 g or less (F), 23 g or less (M)
Cholesterol	174 mg	300 mg or less
Sodium	597 mg	2,400 mg or less
Carbohydrates	30 g	250 g or more
Protein	9 g	55 g to 90 g

NOTES

DOUBLE ONION AND TOMATO TART

We've put together a duet of sweet yellow onions and leeks with fresh and sun-dried tomatoes in this gorgeous harvest tart. Choose from sun-dried tomatoes packaged dried and loose, or bottled in jars with oil or herbs and seasonings.

Prep time: 1 hour
Cooking time: 40 minutes
● *Degree of difficulty: moderate*

Savory Tart Pastry (recipe, page 9)
- 2 **tablespoons butter (no substitutions)**
- 1¼ **pounds onions, thinly sliced**
- 1¼ **pounds leeks (white and pale green parts), thinly sliced**
- 1 **teaspoon minced garlic**
- ¾ **teaspoon salt**
- ¼ **teaspoon thyme**
- ¼ **teaspoon freshly ground pepper**
- ¼ **cup sun-dried tomatoes**
- 1 **plum tomato, thinly sliced**
- ¼ **cup freshly grated Parmesan cheese**
- ¼ **teaspoon freshly cracked pepper**

1 Prepare Savory Tart Pastry as directed.

2 On a lightly floured surface with a floured rolling pin, roll pastry into an ⅛-inch-thick circle and fit into a 9½-inch tart pan with a removable bottom or a 9-inch pie plate. Gently press pastry with fingertips along bottom and up side of pan. With scissors, trim pastry to 1 inch above edge. Fold overhanging pastry into side of crust and gently press edge up to extend ¼ inch above side of pan. Freeze pastry shell for 15 minutes.

3 Preheat oven to 425°F. Line frozen pastry shell with foil and fill with dried beans or uncooked rice. Place on a cookie sheet and bake for 15 minutes. Remove foil and beans. Bake pastry for 5 to 10 minutes more or until golden.

4 Meanwhile, melt the butter in a large skillet over medium-high heat. Add the onions, leeks, garlic, salt, thyme, and ground pepper. Cover and cook, stirring occasionally, for 20 minutes. Uncover and cook for 20 minutes more or until vegetables are very tender and golden.

5 While onions are cooking, pour boiling water over the dried tomatoes in a small bowl. Let stand 5 minutes, then drain and chop. (If using sun-dried tomatoes packed in oil, drain and chop.) Stir tomatoes into onion mixture.

6 Spoon onion and tomato mixture into baked pastry shell. Arrange overlapping slices of plum tomato over the top, then sprinkle with Parmesan cheese and cracked pepper. Bake for 10 minutes. Serve warm or at room temperature. Makes 8 servings.

PER SERVING		DAILY GOAL
Calories	285	2,000 (F), 2,500 (M)
Total fat	13 g	60 g or less (F), 70 g or less (M)
Saturated fat	7 g	20 g or less (F), 23 g or less (M)
Cholesterol	26 mg	300 mg or less
Sodium	508 mg	2,400 mg or less
Carbohydrates	36 g	250 g or more
Protein	6 g	55 g to 90 g

NOTES

_____

_____

_____

_____

_____

_____

_____

FRESH TOMATO TART

A refreshing, light meal for a summer's eve—all you need with it is a green salad and chilled dry white wine. Coating the tomatoes with Parmesan helps absorb the moisture that they give off during baking. *Also pictured on page 108.*

> *Prep time: 25 minutes plus chilling*
> *Baking time: 1 hour*
> ● *Degree of difficulty: moderate*

Savory Tart Pastry (recipe, page 9)
1 **container (15 ounces) ricotta cheese**
3 **large eggs, lightly beaten**
1 **tablespoon chopped fresh oregano** *or* **¼ teaspoon dried oregano mixed with 1 tablespoon chopped fresh parsley**
¾ **teaspoon salt**
¼ **teaspoon freshly ground pepper**
½ **cup freshly grated Parmesan cheese**
2 **medium tomatoes (1¼ pounds), thinly sliced**

1 Prepare Savory Tart Pastry as directed.

2 Preheat oven to 425°F. On a lightly floured surface with a floured rolling pin, roll pastry into an 11-inch circle and fit into a 9-inch pie pan, letting pastry overhang edge. Trim and flute the edge. Freeze for 10 minutes.

3 Line frozen pastry shell with foil and fill with dried beans or uncooked rice. Bake for 10 minutes. Remove foil and beans. Bake pastry for 5 to 10 minutes more or until golden. Cool completely on a wire rack.

4 Reduce oven temperature to 350°F. Combine the ricotta, eggs, oregano, salt, and pepper in a large bowl. Spread the Parmesan on a sheet of wax paper, then coat both sides of tomato slices with cheese. Spread half the ricotta mixture in baked pastry shell and top with half the tomatoes. Cover with remaining ricotta and tomatoes. Bake about 1 hour or until just golden and set. Cool on a wire rack 20 minutes before cutting. Serve warm or at room temperature. Makes 6 servings.

PER SERVING		DAILY GOAL
Calories	430	2,000 (F), 2,500 (M)
Total fat	26 g	60 g or less (F), 70 g or less (M)
Saturated fat	14 g	20 g or less (F), 23 g or less (M)
Cholesterol	168 mg	300 mg or less
Sodium	759 mg	2,400 mg or less
Carbohydrates	31 g	250 g or more
Protein	18 g	55 g to 90 g

NOTES

EGGPLANT-TOMATO TART

Slender Japanese eggplant and plum tomatoes make for a wonderful flavor combination in this tart from Greens restaurant in San Francisco.

Prep time: 40 minutes plus chilling
Baking time: 60 minutes
● *Degree of difficulty: moderate*

Savory Tart Pastry (recipe, page 9)
¼ **cup olive oil**
2 **Japanese eggplants (about 12 ounces total), cut into ⅜-inch-thick slices**
¾ **teaspoon salt**
¾ **teaspoon freshly ground pepper**
2 **large eggs**
1 **large egg yolk**
1 **cup half-and-half *or* light cream**
Pinch nutmeg
½ **cup julienned basil leaves**
½ **cup shredded provolone cheese**
3 **plum tomatoes, peeled, seeded and cut into ⅜-inch-thick slices**

1 Prepare Savory Tart Pastry as directed.

2 On a lightly floured surface with a floured rolling pin, roll pastry into an ⅛-inch-thick circle and fit into a 9½-inch tart pan with a removable bottom or a 9-inch pie plate. Gently press pastry with fingertips along bottom and up side of pan. With scissors, trim pastry to 1 inch above edge. Fold overhanging pastry into side of crust and gently press edge up to extend ¼ inch above side of pan. Freeze pastry shell for 15 minutes.

3 Preheat oven to 425°F. Line pastry shell with foil and fill with dried beans or uncooked rice. Bake for 10 minutes. Remove foil and beans. Bake pastry for 5 minutes more or until pale golden. Cool completely on wire rack.

4 Lightly oil a cookie sheet. Arrange the eggplant slices on cookie sheet in a single layer and brush generously with oil. Sprinkle lightly with the salt and pepper. Bake about 5 minutes or until golden and tender.

5 Beat together the whole eggs, egg yolk, cream, and nutmeg. Sprinkle the basil and cheese over baked pastry shell. Layer eggplant and tomato slices over cheese, then pour on custard. Place filled pastry shell on the lowest oven rack. Bake for 10 minutes. Reduce oven temperature to 375°F. Bake for 30 minutes more or until filling is set and golden. Let stand for 10 minutes before serving. Makes 6 servings.

PER SERVING		DAILY GOAL
Calories	450	2,000 (F), 2,500 (M)
Total fat	31 g	60 g or less (F), 70 g or less (M)
Saturated fat	12 g	20 g or less (F), 23 g or less (M)
Cholesterol	148 mg	300 mg or less
Sodium	661 mg	2,400 mg or less
Carbohydrates	32 g	250 g or more
Protein	10 g	55 g to 90 g

POLENTA-CHEESE TART

Prep time: 15 minutes
Baking time: 15 minutes
○ *Degree of difficulty: easy*

1 **can (13¾ *or* 14½ ounces) chicken broth, divided**
¾ **cup yellow cornmeal**
1 **package (8 ounces) shredded part-skim mozzarella cheese**
3 **ounces goat cheese, crumbled**
2 **tablespoons chopped green onion**
½ **teaspoon freshly ground pepper**
¼ **teaspoon thyme**
½ **red pepper, sliced thin**

½ **yellow pepper, sliced thin**
1 **teaspoon olive oil**

1 Preheat oven to 400°F. Bring 1 cup of the chicken broth to a boil in a small saucepan. Combine the remaining broth with the cornmeal until smooth in a small bowl. Add the cornmeal mixture to the boiling broth; reduce heat to medium and cook, stirring constantly, 5 minutes. Spread on bottom and sides of a 9-inch pie plate to form a crust.

2 Combine the mozzarella, goat cheese, green onions, pepper, and thyme in a medium bowl. Spoon evenly into crust, then top with the red and yellow peppers and drizzle with olive oil. Bake 15 minutes. Makes 4 servings.

PER SERVING		DAILY GOAL
Calories	345	2,000 (F), 2,500 (M)
Total fat	18 g	60 g or less (F), 70 g or less (M)
Saturated fat	10 g	20 g or less (F), 23 g or less (M)
Cholesterol	50 mg	300 mg or less
Sodium	887 mg	2,400 mg or less
Carbohydrates	24 g	250 g or more
Protein	21 g	55 g to 90 g

CHESHIRE CHEESE TART

Prep time: 20 minutes
Baking time: 30 minutes
Degree of difficulty: easy

Savory Tart Pastry (recipe, page 9)
4 **ounces baked ham, finely chopped**
1 **teaspoon dry mustard**
6 **ounces Cheshire *or* cheddar cheese, shredded and divided**
1 **large egg**
1 **cup plus 1 tablespoon milk, divided**
2 **tablespoons butter (no substitutions)**
3 **tablespoons all-purpose flour**
4 **large eggs, separated, at room temperature**

1 Prepare Savory Tart Pastry as directed.

2 On a lightly floured surface with a floured rolling pin, roll pastry into an ⅛-inch-thick circle and fit into a 9-inch pie pan, letting pastry overhang edge. Trim and flute edge of pastry.

3 Preheat oven to 400°F. Combine the ham and mustard in a small bowl, then sprinkle along bottom of pastry shell. Top with ½ cup of the cheese. Beat the whole egg with 1 tablespoon of the milk.

4 Heat the remaining 1 cup milk in a small saucepan over medium heat until small bubbles appear around edge of pan. Meanwhile, melt the butter in another small saucepan. Stir in the flour and cook stirring, 2 minutes. Whisk in the hot milk and bring to a boil. Reduce heat and simmer 10 minutes, stirring occasionally. Remove from heat and whisk in the egg yolks and remaining 4 ounces cheese.

5 Beat the egg whites in a medium bowl until stiff peaks form, then fold into cheese mixture with a rubber spatula. Pour filling into shell, then brush edge of pastry shell with egg-milk mixture. Bake about 30 minutes or until crust is golden and filling is set. Cool at least 30 minutes before serving. Makes 8 servings.

PER SERVING		DAILY GOAL
Calories	380	2,000 (F), 2,500 (M)
Total fat	24 g	60 g or less (F), 70 g or less (M)
Saturated fat	12 g	20 g or less (F), 23 g or less (M)
Cholesterol	191 mg	300 mg or less
Sodium	625 mg	2,400 mg or less
Carbohydrates	22 g	250 g or more
Protein	16 g	55 g to 90 g

ASPARAGUS AND GOAT CHEESE TART

Asparagus aficionados will love their favorite vegetable paired with mild goat cheese. This tart reheats well, so you can bake it a day ahead.

Prep time: 30 minutes plus chilling
Baking time: 53 to 55 minutes
Degree of difficulty: moderate

Savory Tart Pastry (recipe, page 9)
¾ **pound fresh asparagus**
¾ **teaspoon salt, divided**
¼ **cup goat cheese, crumbled**
3 **large eggs, lightly beaten**
1 **cup heavy *or* whipping cream**
1 **tablespoon chopped fresh parsley**
¼ **teaspoon tarragon**
¼ **teaspoon freshly ground pepper**

1 Prepare Savory Tart Pastry as directed.

2 Preheat oven to 425°F. On a lightly floured surface with a floured rolling pin, roll pastry into an 11-inch circle and fit into a 9½-inch tart pan with a removable bottom. Gently press pastry with fingertips along bottom and up side of pan. With scissors, trim pastry to 1 inch above edge. Fold overhanging pastry into side of crust and gently press edge up to extend ¼ inch above side of pan. Freeze 15 minutes.

3 Line frozen pastry shell with foil and fill with dried beans or uncooked rice. Bake for 15 minutes. Remove foil and beans. Bake pastry for 8 to 10 minutes more or until deep golden. Cool completely on a wire rack.

4 Reduce oven temperature to 350°F. Trim and peel the asparagus, then cut into 1-inch pieces. Bring a large skillet of water to boil over high heat. Add the asparagus and ½ teaspoon of the salt and cook about 5 minute or until just tender. Drain in a colander, rinsing under cold water; pat dry.

5 Spread asparagus in baked pastry crust and top with the goat cheese. Place on a cookie sheet. Whisk the eggs, cream, parsley, tarragon, the remaining ¼ teaspoon salt, and the pepper in a medium bowl until combined. Pour over tart.

6 Bake tart on cookie sheet about 30 minutes or until filling is just set. Cool on a wire rack for 15 minutes. (Can be made ahead. Cover and refrigerate overnight. Remove side from tart pan and unmold tart; place tart on a cookie sheet. Cut into 8 wedges. Heat in a preheated 400°F. oven, loosely covered with foil, 10 minutes. Uncover and heat 5 to 10 minutes more.) Serve warm. Makes 8 servings.

PER SERVING		DAILY GOAL
Calories	310	2,000 (F), 2,500 (M)
Total fat	24 g	60 g or less (F), 70 g or less (M)
Saturated fat	15 g	20 g or less (F), 23 g or less (M)
Cholesterol	151 mg	300 mg or less
Sodium	295 mg	2,400 mg or less
Carbohydrates	17 g	250 g or more
Protein	7 g	55 g to 90 g

NOTES

_____

_____

_____

_____

_____

_____

AS EASY

AS PIE

Here come the pies that only take minutes to prepare—pies that love a bowl and a spoon. With a single crust on top, there's no need to worry about a soggy bottom. If you like crisp toppings studded with oats and nuts, we can offer you our spicy Apple-Oat Crisp or Bramble Crisp. Or, if a buttery moist cakelike crust is what you're craving, we've got Peach and Sweet Cherry Cobbler or Raspberry-Rhubarb Cobbler.

BRAMBLE CRISP

Bramble is the fruit from a prickly bush such as blackberry or raspberry. We combined blackberries with apples for an even better taste.

Prep time: 20 minutes
Baking time: 1 hour
O *Degree of difficulty: easy*

Topping
½ **cup hazelnuts, toasted and skinned**
⅔ **cup firmly packed brown sugar**
⅔ **cup all-purpose flour**
½ **teaspoon cinnamon**
¼ **cup cold butter *or* margarine,**
      cut up

Filling
5 **cups peeled and sliced Granny**
      Smith apples (4 *or* 5)
3 **cups fresh blackberries**
¼ **cup granulated sugar**
1 **tablespoon all-purpose flour**

1 Preheat oven to 350°F. For topping, process nuts and brown sugar in a food processor until coarsely chopped. Add the flour and cinnamon, pulsing to blend. With machine on, add the butter through the feed tube until combined.

2 For filling, toss the apples, blackberries, sugar, and flour in a large bowl. Spoon fruit mixture into a shallow 2-quart glass baking dish. Crumble topping evenly on top. Bake about 1 hour or until fruit is bubbly and topping is golden. Makes 8 servings.

PER SERVING		DAILY GOAL
Calories	300	2,000 (F), 2,500 (M)
Total fat	11 g	60 g or less (F), 70 g or less (M)
Saturated fat	4 g	20 g or less (F), 23 g or less (M)
Cholesterol	16 mg	300 mg or less
Sodium	66 mg	2,400 mg or less
Carbohydrates	51 g	250 g or more
Protein	3 g	55 g to 90 g

NOTES

RHUBARB CRISP

A hallmark of the Union Square Cafe, in New York City, is creative, seasonal food prepared by chef Michael Romano. Made with fresh rhubarb at its peak, this simple crisp is the height of springtime splendor.

Prep time: 15 minutes
Baking time: 35 to 40 minutes
○ *Degree of difficulty: easy*

Filling
2 pounds fresh rhubarb, cut into ½-inch pieces (10 cups), *or* 2 bags (16 *or* 20 ounces each) frozen rhubarb
¾ cup granulated sugar
2 tablespoons all-purpose flour

Topping
½ cup butter, softened (no substitutions)
½ cup firmly packed brown sugar
2 tablespoons granulated sugar
1½ cups all-purpose flour
⅛ teaspoon cinnamon
½ cup chopped walnuts, toasted
Vanilla ice cream (optional)

1 Preheat oven to 400°F. For filling, combine the rhubarb, sugar, and flour in a large bowl, tossing to coat well. Transfer to a 10-inch deep-dish pie plate.

2 For topping, beat the butter and both sugars in a large mixing bowl until creamy. Stir in the flour and cinnamon until blended. Stir in the walnuts. Crumble the topping over the rhubarb.

3 Place the crisp on a foil-lined cookie sheet. Bake for 35 to 40 minutes or until filling is bubbly and topping is golden brown. Cool slightly and serve with vanilla ice cream, if desired. Makes 8 servings.

PER SERVING WITHOUT ICE CREAM		DAILY GOAL
Calories	400	2,000 (F), 2,500 (M)
Total fat	17 g	60 g or less (F), 70 g or less (M)
Saturated fat	8 g	0 g or less (F), 23 g or less (M)
Cholesterol	31 mg	300 mg or less
Sodium	128 mg	2,400 mg or less
Carbohydrates	61 g	250 g or more
Protein	5 g	55 g to 90 g

THE RIGHT SPICE

All your favorite spices for pie baking—cinnamon, ginger, nutmeg, cloves, and allspice—should be stored in tightly sealed containers away from heat and light. Properly stored, ground spices should keep up to a year, but always test them for flavor by tasting them or by smelling them for a fresh and pungent aroma before using.

NOTES

_____

_____

_____

_____

_____

_____

APPLE-OAT CRISP

Each apple suggested gives this recipe a slightly different flavor.

Prep time: 15 minutes
Baking time: 40 minutes
○ *Degree of difficulty: easy*

Filling
¼ **cup granulated sugar**
1 **teaspoon cinnamon**
½ **teaspoon ginger**
 Pinch salt
4 **pounds tart apples (Granny Smith, Jonathan, *or* Pippin), peeled, cored, and cut into 8 wedges each**
2 **teaspoons fresh lemon juice**

Oat Topping
⅔ **cup all-purpose flour**
⅔ **cup packed brown sugar**
½ **cup cold butter *or* margarine, cut up**
⅔ **cup old-fashioned oats, uncooked**
⅔ **cup chopped walnuts *or* pecans**
 Vanilla ice cream (optional)

1 Preheat oven to 375°F. For the filling, combine the sugar, cinnamon, ginger, and salt in a large bowl. Add the apples and lemon juice, tossing to coat. Arrange the fruit in an even layer in a shallow 3-quart glass baking dish.

2 For Oat Topping, combine the flour and brown sugar in a medium bowl. With a pastry blender or 2 knives, cut in the butter until mixture resembles coarse crumbs. Stir in the oats and walnuts.

3 Sprinkle apple mixture with Oat Topping. Bake about 40 minutes or until bubbly. Serve warm with vanilla ice cream, if desired. Makes 8 servings.

PER SERVING
WITHOUT ICE CREAM | | DAILY GOAL

Calories	430	2,000 (F), 2,500 (M)
Total fat	19 g	60 g or less (F), 70 g or less (M)
Saturated fat	8 g	20 g or less (F), 23 g or less (M)
Cholesterol	31 mg	300 mg or less
Sodium	140 mg	2,400 mg or less
Carbohydrates	67 g	250 g or more
Protein	3 g	55 g to 90 g

LOVE THEM OATS
Uncooked old-fashioned or quick cooking oats can be used interchangeably in our deep-dish spoon pies and streusel toppings. Instant oats or oatmeal are not good substitutes.

NOTES

SPICED APPLE CRISP

Thanks to the microwave, we've turned spiced apples into a guilt-free crisp with just a sprinkle of gingersnaps.

Ⓜ *Microwave*
▼ *Low-Fat*
▽ *Low-Calorie*
   Prep time: 10 minutes
○ *Degree of difficulty: easy*

4   **medium (7 ounces each) McIntosh apples**
⅓   **cup fresh orange juice**
¼   **teaspoon grated orange peel**
1   **teaspoon cinnamon**
3   **tablespoons firmly packed dark brown sugar**
¼   **cup crushed gingersnap cookies**

1 Peel and core the apples. Slice into ¼-inch-thick rings and arrange in a 10-inch microwave-proof plate. Drizzle the orange juice evenly over top. Mix the orange peel, cinnamon, and sugar in a small bowl and sprinkle over apple slices.

2 Cover dish loosely with wax paper and microwave on high (100% power) for 2 minutes. Rotate dish and microwave 1 to 2 minutes more or until apples are tender. Top with the crushed gingersnaps and serve immediately. Makes 4 servings.

PER SERVING		DAILY GOAL
Calories	170	2,000 (F), 2,500 (M)
Total fat	1 g	60 g or less (F), 70 g or less (M)
Saturated fat	0 g	20 g or less (F), 23 g or less (M)
Cholesterol	0 mg	300 mg or less
Sodium	39 mg	2,400 mg or less
Carbohydrates	42 g	250 g or more
Protein	1 g	55 g to 90 g

NECTARINE-PECAN CRISP

Here's a summery fruit crisp that can be assembled ahead, then baked when guests come to call.

   Prep time: 20 minutes
   Baking time: 25 to 30 minutes
○ *Degree of difficulty: easy*

Filling
5   **pounds ripe nectarines, sliced**
2   **to 3 tablespoons granulated sugar**
1   **tablespoon fresh lemon juice**

Pecan-Oat Topping
¾   **cup firmly packed brown sugar**
½   **cup all-purpose flour**
1   **teaspoon cinnamon**
6   **tablespoons butter *or* margarine, cut up**
¾   **cup rolled oats, uncooked**
¾   **cup chopped pecans, toasted**

1 Preheat oven to 375°F. Butter a 13x9-inch baking dish. For filling, combine the nectarines, sugar, and lemon juice in a large bowl. Spoon into prepared dish. (Can be made ahead. Cover and refrigerate up to 4 hours.)

2 For Pecan-Oat Topping, combine the brown sugar, flour, and cinnamon in a large bowl. With a pastry blender or 2 knives, cut in the butter until mixture resembles coarse crumbs. Stir in the oats and pecans. (Can be made ahead. Cover and refrigerate up to 24 hours.)

3 Sprinkle topping evenly over fruit. Bake for 25 to 30 minutes or until fruit is bubbly. (If topping browns too quickly, cover loosely with foil.) Serve warm. Makes 12 servings.

PER SERVING		DAILY GOAL
Calories	260	2,000 (F), 2,500 (M)
Total fat	11 g	60 g or less (F), 70 g or less (M)
Saturated fat	4 g	20 g or less (F), 23 g or less (M)
Cholesterol	16 mg	300 mg or less
Sodium	68 mg	2,400 mg or less
Carbohydrates	41 g	250 g or more
Protein	3 g	55 g to 90 g

CINNAMON-VANILLA CUSTARD SAUCE

Prep time: 10 minutes plus chilling
Cooking time: 10 minutes
● *Degree of difficulty: moderate*

1 **vanilla bean** *or* 1 **teaspoon**
    vanilla extract
1¼ **cups milk**
1 **cinnamon stick**
3 **large egg yolks**
¼ **cup granulated sugar**

1 Split the vanilla bean in half lengthwise and scrape out seeds. Place pod and seeds in small saucepan with the milk and cinnamon stick. Bring mixture to a boil.

2 Meanwhile, whisk the egg yolks and sugar together in a small bowl. Gradually whisk in hot milk. Return to saucepan and cook, stirring constantly, over medium heat about 5 minutes or until mixture thickens slightly and coats the back of a spoon. *(Do not boil.)* Strain through a fine sieve into a medium bowl, discarding vanilla pod and cinnamon stick. Refrigerate for 2 hours or until cold. Makes 1⅓ cups.

PER TABLESPOON		DAILY GOAL
Calories	30	2,000 (F), 2,500 (M)
Total Fat	1 g	60 g or less (F), 70 g or less (M)
Saturated fat	5 g	20 g or less (F), 23 g or less (M)
Cholesterol	32 mg	300 mg or less
Sodium	8 mg	2,400 mg or less
Carbohydrates	3 g	250 g or more
Protein	1 g	55 g to 90 g

PIES WITH THE BEST ZEST

When choosing a lemon, lime, or orange for grated peel, look for firm, thick-skinned fruit. Place a four-sided grater on a sheet of wax paper. Using the fine side of the grater, grate only the colored outer peel, leaving the bitter white pith on the fruit. Use a rubber spatula to scrape up any peel stuck to the grater.

NOTES

135

RASPBERRY-RHUBARB COBBLER

For the best flavor in this homey fruit dessert, use real maple syrup. *Also pictured on page 128.*

Prep time: 25 to 30 minutes
Baking time: 15 to 20 minutes
O *Degree of difficulty: easy*

Topping
¾ cup chopped pecans
½ cup biscuit baking mix
½ cup firmly packed brown sugar
3 tablespoons butter *or* margarine, melted

Filling
1½ cups fresh raspberries
1½ cups sliced fresh rhubarb
¾ cup pure maple syrup *or* ½ cup pancake syrup
1 tablespoon cornstarch
¼ cup cold water

Crust
2 cups biscuit baking mix
½ cup heavy *or* whipping cream
3 tablespoons butter *or* margarine, melted
1½ tablespoons granulated sugar

1 Preheat oven to 400°F. Grease a 9-inch square baking pan.

2 For topping, combine the pecans, baking mix, brown sugar, and butter in a medium bowl. Set aside.

3 For filling, combine the raspberries, rhubarb, and syrup in a medium saucepan. Cook, stirring frequently, over medium heat for 5 to 10 minutes or until rhubarb is tender. Dissolve the cornstarch in cold water, then stir into fruit mixture. Boil, stirring constantly, for 2 minutes.

4 For crust, combine the baking mix, cream, butter, and sugar in a medium bowl. Pat into the prepared pan. Pour fruit over crust. Crumble the topping over the fruit. Bake for 15 to 20 minutes or until fruit is bubbly and topping is golden. Serve warm. Makes 8 servings.

PER SERVING		DAILY GOAL
Calories	495	2,000 (F), 2,500 (M)
Total fat	25 g	60 g or less (F), 70 g or less (M)
Saturated fat	10 g	20 g or less (F), 23 g or less (M)
Cholesterol	45 mg	300 mg or less
Sodium	540 mg	2,400 mg or less
Carbohydrates	65 g	250 g or more
Protein	4 g	55 g to 90 g

NOTES

_____
_____
_____
_____
_____
_____
_____
_____
_____
_____
_____
_____
_____

137

TRUE BLUEBERRY COBBLER

Prep time: 20 minutes
Baking time: 20 to 25 minutes
○ *Degree of difficulty: easy*

Filling
- 5 cups fresh blueberries
- ¾ cup granulated sugar
- 2 tablespoons water
- 2 tablespoons cornstarch
- ¼ teaspoon cinnamon
- 2 tablespoons fresh lemon juice
- ½ teaspoon grated lemon peel

Topping
- 2 tablespoons granulated sugar, divided
- ⅛ teaspoon cinnamon
  Pinch nutmeg
- 1 cup all-purpose flour
- 1½ teaspoons baking powder
- ⅛ teaspoon salt
- ¼ cup cold butter *or* margarine, cut up
- ½ cup heavy *or* whipping cream
  Vanilla ice cream (optional)

1 Preheat oven to 425°F. For filling, combine the blueberries, sugar, water, cornstarch, and cinnamon in a large saucepan. Bring to a boil, stirring constantly, 1 minute. Stir in the lemon juice and peel. Pour mixture into a 9-inch square baking pan. Cover and keep warm.

2 For topping, combine 1 tablespoon of the sugar, cinnamon, and nutmeg in a small bowl; set aside. Combine the flour, remaining 1 tablespoon sugar, baking powder, and salt in a large bowl. Cut in the butter until mixture resembles coarse crumbs. Stir in the cream just until blended. Knead just until mixture holds together. On a lightly floured surface, pat dough into a 9-inch square. Place over hot berry mixture and sprinkle with reserved sugar-spice mixture.

3 Place on a cookie sheet and bake 20 to 25 minutes or until golden. Serve warm with vanilla ice cream, if desired. Serves 6.

PER SERVING WITHOUT ICE CREAM		DAILY GOAL
Calories	405	2,000 (F), 2,500 (M)
Total fat	16 g	60 g or less (F), 70 g or less (M)
Saturated fat	9 g	20 g or less (F), 23 g or less (M)
Cholesterol	48 mg	300 mg or less
Sodium	262 mg	2,400 mg or less
Carbohydrates	66 g	250 g or more
Protein	3 g	55 g to 90 g

APPLE-PEAR BROWN BETTY

Prep time: 25 minutes
Baking time: 60 minutes
○ *Degree of difficulty: easy*

- 3 Granny Smith apples, peeled and thinly sliced
- 3 ripe pears, peeled and thinly sliced
- 1 tablespoon fresh lemon juice
- 5 slices whole wheat bread, cubed
- ¼ cup butter *or* margarine, melted
- 1 tablespoon granulated sugar
- ⅔ cup firmly packed brown sugar
- ½ teaspoon grated lemon peel
- ¼ teaspoon cinnamon
- ⅛ teaspoon nutmeg
  Cinnamon-Vanilla Custard Sauce (recipe, page 135)

1 Preheat oven to 375°F. Toss the apples and pears with the lemon juice in a large bowl. Toss the bread cubes with the butter and granulated sugar in a medium bowl. Combine the brown sugar, lemon peel, cinnamon, and nutmeg in another bowl.

2 Spread half the fruit mixture in a buttered, 9-inch square baking dish. Sprinkle with half the bread cubes then half the brown sugar mixture; repeat layering. Cover and bake for 30 minutes. Uncover and bake for 30 minutes more or until top is golden and fruit is bubbly. Serve with Cinnamon-Vanilla Custard Sauce. Makes 6 servings.

PER SERVING WITHOUT SAUCE		DAILY GOAL
Calories	405	2,000 (F), 2,500 (M)
Total fat	13 g	60 g or less (F), 70 g or less (M)
Saturated fat	7 g	20 g or less (F), 23 g or less (M)
Cholesterol	134 mg	300 mg or less
Sodium	228 mg	2,400 mg or less
Carbohydrates	70 g	250 g or more
Protein	5 g	55 g to 90 g

APPLE COBBLER

A bit more elegant than most cobblers, this warm apple dessert from Aspen, Colorado's luxury resort, The Little Nell, will remind you of the classic French Tarte Tatin.

Prep time: 30 minutes plus chilling
Cooking time: 1 hour
Baking Time: 20 minutes
Degree of difficulty: moderate

Pastry
2   cups all-purpose flour
¼   cup granulated sugar
1   teaspoon salt
⅓   cup cold butter, cut up (no substitutions)
⅓   cup vegetable shortening
3   to 4 tablespoons ice water

Filling
¾   cup butter, cut up, divided
1   cup granulated sugar, divided
12   Golden Delicious apples (about 5 pounds)
    Sweetened whipped cream (optional)

1 For pastry, combine the flour, sugar, and salt. Gradually add butter and shortening, tossing until pieces are coated with flour. Cut in butter and shortening until mixture resembles coarse crumbs. Add ice water, 1 tablespoon at a time, tossing with a fork until pastry begins to hold together. Shape into a ball, kneading lightly if necessary. Flatten into a thick disk. Wrap and chill 30 minutes or overnight.

2 On a lightly floured surface, roll pastry into a 14-inch circle. Trim to a 13-inch circle. Transfer to a cookie sheet and chill.

3 Preheat oven to 425°F. For filling, add 6 tablespoons of the cut up butter to a heavy, 12-inch oven-proof skillet. Sprinkle ½ cup of the sugar over butter in skillet. *(Wrap the handle of the skillet with foil.)* Peel, halve, and core the apples. Arrange apples on their sides in tight concentric circles in the skillet, packing in as many apples as possible. Sprinkle with remaining butter and sugar. Cook over medium-high heat for 20 to 25 minutes or until apples begin to brown. Carefully turn apples over and cook about 30 minutes more or until juices become dark caramel-colored.

4 Remove skillet from heat and place pastry on top, tucking in edges. Bake about 20 minutes or until pastry is golden. Immediately invert carefully onto a serving platter, rearranging any apples that stick in the skillet. Serve warm or at room temperature with sweetened whipped cream, if desired. Makes 12 servings.

PER SERVING		DAILY GOAL
Calories	445	2,000 (F), 2,500 (M)
Total fat	23 g	60 g or less (F), 70 g or less (M)
Saturated fat	11 g	20 g or less (F), 23 g or less (M)
Cholesterol	45 mg	300 mg or less
Sodium	353 mg	2,400 mg or less
Carbohydrates	60 g	250 g or more
Protein	3 g	55 g to 90 g

PEACH AND SWEET CHERRY COBBLER

The quintessential June dessert: peaches and fresh sweet cherries baked together with a spiced biscuit topping.

Prep time: 30 minutes
Baking time: 20 minutes
Degree of difficulty: easy

Filling
- 6 cups peeled and sliced ripe peaches (3½ pounds)
- 4 cups pitted fresh sweet cherries (2 pounds)
- ¾ cup granulated sugar
- ¼ cup cornstarch
- 3 tablespoons fresh lemon juice

Topping
- 2 cups all-purpose flour
- ⅓ cup plus 2 tablespoons granulated sugar, divided
- 2½ teaspoons baking powder
- ½ teaspoon salt
- ½ cup cold butter *or* margarine, cut up
- ¾ cup plus 2 tablespoons heavy *or* whipping cream, divided
- ¼ teaspoon cinnamon
- Vanilla ice cream (optional)

1 Preheat oven to 425°F. Grease a 13x9-inch glass or ceramic baking dish.

2 For filling, combine the peaches, cherries, sugar, and cornstarch in a large saucepan. Bring to a boil, stirring gently, over high heat and boil 1 minute. Remove from heat, then stir in the lemon juice. Spoon into prepared dish.

3 For topping, combine the flour, ⅓ cup of the sugar, the baking powder, and salt in a large bowl. With a pastry blender or 2 knives, cut in the butter until mixture resembles coarse crumbs. Stir in ¾ cup of the cream. Knead 2 or 3 times, just until dough holds together. On a floured surface with a floured rolling pin, roll dough to ½-inch thick. Cut with 2½- or 3-inch decorative cookie cutters, re-rolling scraps. Place biscuits over fruit.

4 Combine the remaining 2 tablespoons sugar, the remaining 2 tablespoons cream, and the cinnamon in a cup and brush over biscuits. Bake for 20 minutes or until fruit is bubbly and biscuits are golden. Let stand for 10 minutes. (Can be made ahead. Let stand up to 2 hours.) Serve with vanilla ice cream, if desired. Makes 10 servings.

PER SERVING WITHOUT ICE CREAM		DAILY GOAL
Calories	465	2,000 (F), 2,500 (M)
Total fat	18 g	60 g or less (F), 70 g or less (M)
Saturated fat	11 g	20 g or less (F), 23 g or less (M)
Cholesterol	53 mg	300 mg or less
Sodium	334 mg	2,400 mg or less
Carbohydrates	74 g	250 g or more
Protein	5 g	55 g to 90 g

NOTES

INDEX

METRIC COOKING HINTS

By making a few conversions, cooks in Australia, Canada, and the United Kingdom can use the recipes in Ladies' Home Journal® *100 Great Pie & Pastry Recipes* with confidence. The charts on this page provide a guide for converting measurements from the U.S. customary system, which is used throughout this book, to the imperial and metric systems. There also is a conversion table for oven temperatures to accommodate the differences in oven calibrations.

Volume and Weight: Americans traditionally use cup measures for liquid and solid ingredients. The chart (top right) shows the approximate imperial and metric equivalents. If you are accustomed to weighing solid ingredients, here are some helpful approximate equivalents.
- 1 cup butter, caster sugar, or rice = 8 ounces = about 250 grams
- 1 cup flour = 4 ounces = about 125 grams
- 1 cup icing sugar = 5 ounces = about 150 grams

Spoon measures are used for smaller amounts of ingredients. Although the size of the tablespoon varies slightly among countries, for practical purposes and for recipes in this book, a straight substitution is all that's necessary.

Measurements made using cups or spoons should always be level, unless stated otherwise.

Product Differences: Most of the ingredients called for in the recipes in this book are available in English-speaking countries. However, some are known by different names. Here are some common American ingredients and their possible counterparts:
- Sugar is granulated or caster sugar.
- Confectioners' sugar is icing sugar.
- All-purpose flour is plain household flour or white flour. When self-rising flour is used in place of all-purpose flour in a recipe that calls for leavening, omit the leavening agent (baking soda or baking powder) and salt.
- Light corn syrup is golden syrup.
- Cornstarch is cornflour.
- Baking soda is bicarbonate of soda.
- Vanilla is vanilla essence.
- Green, red or yellow sweet peppers are capsicums.
- Sultanas are golden raisins.

USEFUL EQUIVALENTS: U.S. = AUST./BR.

⅛ teaspoon = 0.5 ml
¼ teaspoon = 1 ml
½ teaspoon = 2 ml
1 teaspoon = 5 ml
1 tablespoon = 1 tablespoon
¼ cup = 2 tablespoons = 2 fluid ounces = 60 ml
⅓ cup = ¼ cup = 3 fluid ounces = 90 ml
½ cup = ⅓ cup = 4 fluid ounces = 120 ml

⅔ cup = ½ cup = 5 fluid ounces = 150 ml
¾ cup = ⅔ cup = 6 fluid ounces = 180 ml
1 cup = ¾ cup = 8 fluid ounces = 240 ml
1¼ cups = 1 cup
2 cups = 1 pint
1 quart = 1 litre
½ inch = 1.27 centimetres
1 inch = 2.54 centimetres

BAKING PAN SIZES

American	Metric
8x1½-inch round baking pan	20x4-centimetre cake tin
9x1½-inch round baking pan	23x3.5-centimetre cake tin
11x7x1½-inch baking pan	28x18x4-centimetre baking pan
13x9x2-inch baking pan	30x20x3-centimetre baking pan
2-quart rectangular baking dish	30x20x3-centimetre baking pan
15x10x2-inch baking pan	38x25.5x2-centimetre baking pan (Swiss roll tin)
9-inch pie plate	22x4- or 23x4-centimetre pie plate
7- or 8-inch springform pan	18- or 20-centimetre springform or loose-bottom cake tin
9x5x3-inch loaf pan	23x13x7-centimetre or 2-pound narrow loaf tin or paté tin
1½-quart casserole	1.5-litre casserole
2-quart casserole	2-litre casserole

OVEN TEMPERATURE EQUIVALENTS

Fahrenheit Setting	Celsius Setting*	Gas Setting
300°F	150°C	Gas Mark 2
325°F	160°C	Gas Mark 3 (moderately slow)
350°F	180°C	Gas Mark 4 (moderate)
375°F	190°C	Gas Mark 5 (moderately hot)
400°F	200°C	Gas Mark 6 (hot)
425°F	220°C	Gas Mark 7
450°F	230°C	Gas Mark 8 (very hot)
Broil		Grill

Electric and gas ovens may be calibrated using Celsius. However, increase the Celsius setting 10 to 20 degrees when cooking above 160°C with an electric oven. For convection or forced-air ovens (gas or electric), lower the temperature setting 10°C when cooking at all heat levels.